Diagram Diaries

PETER EISENMAN

PETER EISENMAN

DIAGRAM DIARIES

UNIVERSE

First published in the United States of America in 1999
by UNIVERSE PUBLISHING
A Division of Rizzoli International Publications, Inc.
300 Park Avenue South
New York, NY 10010

01 02 03 04 / 10 9 8 7 6 5 4 3 2

Library of Congress Cataloging-in-Publication Data
Eisenman, Peter.
  Diagram diaries / Peter Eisenman ; introduction by R.E. Somol.
  p.   cm.
  ISBN 9-7893-0264-0 (alk. paper)
  1. Eisenman, Peter—Contributions in architectural design. I. Title.
II. Title: Diagram diaries.
NA787.E33A4 1999
720.92—DC21   99–10846

Printed in Italy

Design by Juliette Cezzar

Contents

Dummy Text, or The Diagrammatic Basis of Contemporary Architecture

R.E. Somol

Peter Eisenman has often remarked that his Ph.D. thesis of 1963, "The Formal Basis of Modern Architecture," was a critical response to Christopher Alexander's earlier Cambridge dissertation, which would be published as *Notes on the Synthesis of Form*.[1] While the architectural agendas announced by these projects could not be more dissimilar—determining the "fitness of form" as a problem of set theory versus releasing the potential for forms to notate the forces of their emergence—it should not be overlooked that the techniques of diagramming are central to each. In fact, Alexander begins the 1971 preface to *Notes* by baldly stating that the most significant contribution of his book is "the idea of the diagrams." In some ways, the present collection, *Diagram Diaries*, advances a related assertion, a post-facto preface to an unpublished dissertation, though one that now addresses (and is demonstrated by) a career-long body of intervening work.

In general, the fundamental technique and procedure of architectural knowledge has seemingly shifted, over the second half of the twentieth century, from the drawing to the diagram. This is not to suggest that a diagram of one form or another was not always constitutive of architecture at various points in its history, but simply that it has only been in the last thirty years or so that the diagram has become fully "actualized," that it has become almost completely the *matter* of architecture. Proceeding with halting steps through serial obsessions with form, language, and representation—though, as will be seen, equally with program, force, and performance—the diagram has seemingly emerged as the final tool, in both its millennial and desperate guises, for architectural production and discourse. Relatively impervious to the specific ideology being promoted, the diagram has instigated a range of contemporary

practices. Just as Robert Venturi summarized the effect of his 1950 M.A. thesis as "one great diagram," Lawrence Halprin published a book of diagrams in 1970—which he referred to as "scores"—intended to form the foundation of a renewed design discipline. Significantly, even Klaus Herdeg's critique of the Bauhaus-inspired diagram of pedagogy and design at the Harvard Graduate School of Design proceeded simply through an alternative form of diagrammatic analysis.

It should not be surprising that the discourse of the diagram at this moment has become so confused given its near-universal use and abuse, its simultaneous promotion and denigration. This was less true with the previous trait of disciplinary identity, the act of drawing (*disegno*), which, as Reyner Banham writes, "had such a crucial value for architects that being unable to think without drawing became the true mark of one fully socialized into the profession of architecture."[2] With the increasing inability after the war to link convincingly the formal and functional ambitions of modernism, the first appearances of the diagram solidify around two possible axes, which Colin Rowe would later identify as "paradigm" (the embrace of *a priori* ideals) and "program" (the empirical solicitation of facts). While Rowe significantly notes that both positions "condemn us to no more than simple repetition," he ultimately endorses the side of paradigm (or type) and suggests, true to his predilection for a Renaissance humanism, that it is precisely the drawing that will overcome the diagrammatic alternatives he so ably identifies but too quickly dismisses.[3] In lieu of a return to drawing and modified types, however, an alternative version of repetition (a potentially non-linear mode of repetition) has more recently been pursued by rethinking and extending the logic of the diagram. Thus, the rise of the diagram, a more polemical device than the drawing, accompanies a breakdown of the post-Renaissance consensus on the role of the architect, and achieves its apotheosis with the emergence of the "information architects" (or architect-critics) after 1960. This latter association begins to suggest that not all recent uses of the diagram are equally "diagrammatic."

As the dominant device within the hybrid practices of the architect-critics of the neo–avant-garde, this more specific use of the diagram promises to elide Rowe's postwar opposition between *physique-form* and *morale-word*. Whereas Rowe would elevate the former pair over the latter in his attempt to extend the legacy of modernism (in contrast to his alter ego, Banham, who would elaborate the implications of the second pair), the architects of the neo–avant-garde are drawn to the diagram because— unlike drawing or text, *partis pris* or bubble notation—it appears in the first instance to operate precisely *between* form and word. For the purposes of this brief introduction, this attitude toward the diagram has several implications: that it is fundamentally a *disciplinary* device in that it situates itself on and undoes specific institutional and discursive oppositions (and that it provides a projective discipline for new work); that it suggests an alternative mode of

repetition (one which deviates from the work of the modernist avant-gardes and envisions repetition as the production of difference rather than identity); and that it is a performative rather than a representational device (i.e., it is a tool of the virtual rather than the real). For an early version of this new disciplinary role inscribed in a project, one can look, for example, to Robert Venturi's National Football Hall of Fame Competition entry (or so-called "Billdingboard," 1967), which consists of a tripartite division of the "billboard" entrance facade, a vaulted exhibition shed, and a sloped grandstand in the rear. What one reads in section—from the slightly inclined seating, through the arc of the shed's roof, to the armature of the upright facade—is the 90 degree rotation of a horizontal surface (a table or drafting board) into a vertical object. As with John Hejduk's Wall Houses, Venturi's competition entry describes the transformation of the horizontal space of writing into the vertical surface of the visual, Rowe's *morale-word* becoming *physique-flesh*, a process that diagrams a new professional identification which collapses writing and design.[4] Venturi's appropriation of this swinging tabletop—a drafting room appliance that evinces the documentary status of the discipline—recalls Corbusier's similar use of industrial ready-mades (e.g., the file cabinet, bottle

rack, ocean liner, briar pipe, etc.) as the basis for new organizing systems in the Unités and other projects. The drafting board itself (and here Venturi refers to the front elevation as a "high easel") becomes used as a *diagram*, one which mobilizes a series of relations and forces. Moreover, by proceeding through a misreading of Corbusier's proto-machinic or diagrammatic disposition, the project also suggests that an alternative mode of repetition might be available to architecture, one distinct from the equal but opposite functional and formal reconstructions of modernism after the war.

The history of architectural production over the last forty years can broadly be characterized as the desire to establish an architecture at once *autonomous* and *heterogeneous* in contrast to the *anonymous* and *homogenous* building associated with the interwar rhetoric and postwar experience of the modern movement. This quest for autonomy and heterogeneity—with its fundamental antinomy in the call for both identity and multiplicity—has taken several forms in this period, one of which is a continual misreading or repetition of the modernist avant-gardes, though now in a significantly transformed postwar context. Briefly, then, it might be useful to distinguish between two kinds of repetition, one associated with postmodern historicism and the

other with the constructive swerves, or misreadings, of the neo–avant-garde. The first model of repetition can be identified with icons, resemblances, and copies, while the second is aligned with simulacra or phantasms.[5] The first repetition relies on an ideal of the origin or model, an economy of identity, and can be thought of as typologically driven (the vertical imitation of timeless precedents). In contrast, the second sets in motion divergent series and exists as a continual process of differentiating. One points back to a static moment of being, while the other advances through modes of becoming. Again, this has a direct relation to what Gilles Deleuze also distinguishes as the factitious (or artificial) and the simulacrum:

9

> It is at the core of modernity, at the point where modernism settles its accounts, that the factitious and the simulacrum stand in opposition as two modes of destruction may: the two nihilisms. For between the destruction which conserves and perpetuates the established order of representations, models and copies, and the destruction of models and copies which sets up a creative chaos, there is a great difference; that chaos, which sets in motion the simulacra and raises a phantasm, is the most innocent of all destructions, that of Platonism.[6]

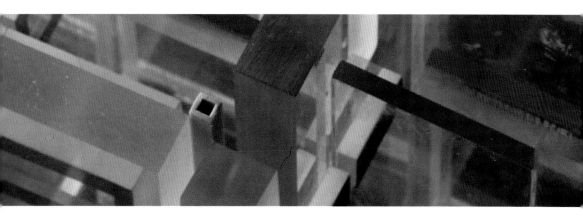

It is now possible to differentiate the repetition of the neo–avant-garde (that of the simulacrum) from the larger trajectory of postmodern historicism, which idealizes the work, stabilizes the referent, and banks on its resemblance. Historicism in this account has little to do with style, but is more a mode of operating, since historicist work can equally include the modern, as evident in the projects of Richard Meier. A particular kind of repetition is at the heart of modernity, however—that of the mis-reading of the avant-garde—and it is this form of practice that relies on the diagram in its fullest sense. Finally, this distinction between modes of repetition provides competing views of "autonomy" as well—i.e., there is the disciplinary autonomy that relies on *typology*, and the alternative call associated with the neo–avant-garde that understands autonomy as a *process* of self-generation or self-organization, a model that allows for formal-material emergence or transformation without authorial intervention, where time is an active rather than a passive element.

As early as his dissertation, Eisenman had implied that the diagrams of Rowe and Alexander (which are more accurately "paradigms" and "patterns," respectively) were insufficiently diagrammatic in that they attempt to represent or identify a static truth condition (whether formal or operational is irrelevant). Advancing the potential of registering site forces and movement via inflections in generic form, Eisenman's transformational diagramming techniques anticipate the need for (and predict the possibilities of) the later development of 3D modeling and animation software. Even in this nascent dynamic construction of the diagram (and non-linear model of repetition), Eisenman imagined that the grid itself could move from an analytic tool of description—the invisible infrastructure of postwar formalism—to a material to be manipulated itself. This approach, of course, was in direct contrast to that of Rowe, who filtered out the wild element of time in favor of timeless resemblance vouchsafed by the stabilizing substrate of an ideal grid.

Rowe's first published essay is a virtuoso performance in formal architectural criticism; it provides a subtle comparison and differentiation of Corbusier's Villa Garches and Palladio's Villa Malcontenta, an analysis that remains both striking and unsettling even now, almost fifty years after its original appearance. Certainly, one can discern the influence on Rowe of Rudolf Wittkower's geometric analysis of Palladio's villas, work which would achieve its definitive statement in Wittkower's *Architectural Principles in the Age of Humanism*, published two years after Rowe's essay. Still, Rowe's lasting contribution,

against all previous understandings, was to cross historical periods and locate a mannerist-humanist project at the *center* of the modern movement, thus establishing a discursive frame through which architectural polemics have been projected ever since—an act that might be described as one of sheer ideological hubris. Moreover, even at this early date, the primary issue revolved around the propriety or appropriateness of "repetition," as suggested in the final two lines of the essay:

> The neo-Palladian villa, at its best, became the picturesque object in the English park and Le Corbusier has become the source of innumerable pastiches and of tediously amusing exhibition techniques; but it is the magnificently realized quality of the originals which one rarely finds in the works of neo-Palladians and exponents of "le style Corbu." These distinctions scarcely require insistence; and no doubt it should only be sententiously suggested that, in the case of derivative works, it is perhaps an adherence to rules which has lapsed.[7]

Though Rowe seems to be distinguishing between two forms of repetition—since the repetition between Palladio and Corbusier is apparently endorsed—the model he defends is still founded on an ideal of "originals." Perhaps more significantly, he alludes here to a legal grounding, the "adherence to rules," to adjudicate cases of repetition, the first of many such invocations of the rule of the law in Rowe's liberal reconstruction of modernism. Also, though critical of the immediate postwar version of *le style Corbu*, twenty-seven years later Rowe would write a brief in support of the New York Five's repetition of Le Corbusier, even if it is, as he confesses, "a largely negative introduction—an attack upon a potential attack," a prime specimen of a slippery-slope logic issued with the sole intention of getting his clients off: "For, in terms of a general theory of pluralism, how can any faults in principle be imputed?"[8] And if one equates Palladio and Le Corbusier, as Rowe's analysis has, then it is logical that he remarks—demonstrating in yet another manner his obsessive attachment to analogical reasoning—that the Five "place themselves in the role, the secondary role, of Scamozzi to Palladio."

In the same year that he issued his somewhat reluctant defense of the New York Five, Rowe wrote an addendum to his "Mathematics" essay that further clarifies his position on repetition. Here, he describes his mode of criticism as "Wölflinian in origin" and says that it "begins with approximate

11

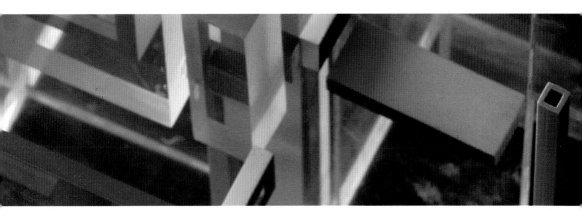

configurations and . . . then proceeds to identify differences."[9] This approach derives from an understanding of repetition in the first sense described above, the one Deleuze associates with the axiom "only that which is alike differs." This mode of *identifying differences* relies on an existing *langue*, or ideal armature, against which seemingly disparate instances like Garches and Malcontenta can be related and distinguished—such that LeCorbusier's emphasis on dispersion and Palladio's on centrality can be defined as viable and coherent options within a larger paradigm—and by which derivative bad copies can be dismissed as falling too far from the proper model.

Such an extension of this model of repetition as a pedagogical project—the intellectual underpinnings of which were largely provided by the "Chicago Frame" and "Transparency" essays—would become officially instituted at the University of Texas in Austin in 1954 with a memorandum ghost-written for Dean Harwell Hamilton Harris by Rowe and Bernard Hoesli.[10] And it is from this curricular framework that, initially in the studios of John Hejduk, the nine-square problem would emerge as perhaps the most durable and widespread beginning design problem in the postwar period.[11] The elegance and ingenuity of this problem lay in the way it consolidated a series of discourses and demands.

Thus, while the technical preconditions that would allow modern architecture to refound itself exclusively on the twin bases of *structure* and *space* had existed for almost a hundred years, the aesthetic, philosophical, and intellectual sources—i.e., the unique combination of cubism, liberalism, gestalt psychology, and the new criticism, with a renewed understanding of mannerist organizing geometries—would not be consolidated as an articulate assemblage until the 1950s, when it would provide a new disciplinary foundation for high modern (or mannerist modern) architectural design and pedagogy. As an educational device, the nine-square problem emerged from a collapse of two modern diagrams—Le Corbusier's domino (*structure*) with van Doesburg's axonometrics (*space*)—filtered through the reductive planimetric logic hypostatized by Wittkower as Palladio's "twelfth villa." What this problem provided was a *discipline* for modern architecture, a perverse and clever argument for a rhetorical capacity against those who would understand modern architecture as simply the literal addition of constructional systems and programmatic requirements. Further, it assumed a *language* of architecture founded on the articulation of a series of dialectics (center and periphery, vertical and horizontal, inside and outside, frontality and rotation, solid and void, point and plane, etc.), a logic

of contradiction and ambiguity. And it is largely to the lessons issuing from Analytic and Synthetic Cubism (and the compositional models of collage emanating from the latter) that Rowe continues to return in his pictorial rendering of the language of modern architecture, an optical bias present even in his assessment of the work of the Five:

> [I]t might be more reasonable and more modest to recognize that, in the opening years of this century, great revolutions in thought occurred and that then profound visual discoveries resulted, that these are still unexplained, and that rather than assume intrinsic change to be the prerogative of every generation, it might be more useful to recognize that certain changes are so enormous as to impose a directive which cannot be resolved in any individual life span. . . . It concerns the plastic and spatial inventions of Cubism and the proposition that, whatever may be said about these, they possess an eloquence and a flexibility which continues now to be as overwhelming as it was then.[12]

This "flexibility" of Cubism and collage provides an institutional and disciplinary basis for architecture beginning with Rowe, while the diverse series of ideal villas and collage cities that derive from this

tradition represent a sustained reflection on the form and content of individual and collective arrangements and an investigation into varied compositional and associative laws in the relation of part-to-whole.

In their dispute with this formalist reconstruction of postwar modernism, the subject of Hejduk's and Eisenman's "anxious influence," to borrow Harold Bloom's model, was first and foremost a strong critic rather than a strong poet. In other words, all of their productive misreadings of modernist European predecessors can be understood as a "swerve" within and against the production of Rowe's formalism, and it is this swerve that allows them to develop other possibilities suppressed within that tradition. In this way, one can read characters from Hejduk's *Vladivostok* or Eisenman's typological field studies from the Rebstockpark Competition as perverse extensions of the gestalt diagrams Rowe and Slutzky used in their second "Transparency" article from 1956. While miming Rowe's sources, however, the projects of Hejduk and Eisenman simultaneously subvert the values of transparency, verticality, opticality, and figure-ground definition that the diagrams were initially rostered to support.

Whereas the separation of space and structure in the nine-square problem enabled one to articulate

13

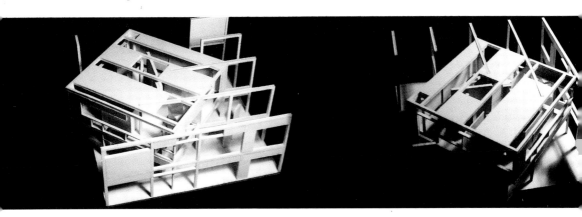

House III

14

formal-plastic relations, the disengagement of the sign from the box in Venturi's "decorated shed" ultimately suggested that these manipulations were unnecessary, as all such relations would be consumed by surface noise. While Rowe and company attempted to replace the neutral, homogenous conception of modernist *space* with the positive figuration of *form*, the neo–avant-garde began to question the stability of form through understanding it as a fictional construct, a *sign*. This semiotic critique would register that form was not a purely visual-optical phenomenon, not "neutral," but constructed by linguistic and institutional relations. Assuming multiple directions, this agenda was first broached in Venturi's particular deployment of a collage practice that was not merely compositional but which would include both text as well as "low" or base references (specific iconic representations). Subsequently, Eisenman's deviation of form would move not to information or the sign (as did Venturi's), but to the trace, the missing index of formal processes (thus stressing absence and the conceptual). At the same time, Hejduk would investigate the theatrical construction of form through highly orchestrated relations and instructions, both linguistic and contractual (i.e., the symbolic). Thus, this three-pronged critique would variously foreground *context* (the framing

mechanisms outside form); *process* (the active procedures within formation); and *usage* (form's relation to a subject). With the neo–avant-garde, then, *form* would be precisely subjected to the functions of its linguistic descendants: in*form*ing, trans*form*ing, and per*form*ing.

For his part, Eisenman develops one of his earliest and most extensive analyses of form by rewriting two structures by the Italian architect Giuseppe Terragni—the Casa del Fascio and the Casa Giuliani-Frigerio—having first encountered this work in the summer of 1961 when he traveled to Como with Rowe. Previous to Eisenman's writings on Terragni, in the late 1950s and early 1960s, Rowe had already developed the terms for a high formalist interpretation of modern architecture, primarily through his elaborate readings of Le Corbusier. Eisenman's contribution to that discourse would be to suspend formal analysis on a structuralist base, a seemingly slight shift in emphasis that would ultimately undermine the way American formalism had institutionalized modernism in the postwar context. In other words, Eisenman was able to transform the discourse from within by appropriating the term "formalism" and deploying it to register the more polemical idea of "work on language" in the Russian formalist sense. This move began to

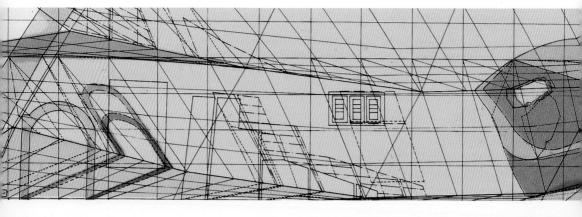

displace the aestheticization of the unique art work that accompanied the Anglo-American version of formalism present in the work of the New Critics, Clement Greenberg, and even Rowe. More generally, Eisenman's project has always entailed a return to the critical aspects of the historical avant-garde, aspects that had been repressed in theory and practice precisely through the formalist reconstruction of modernism after the war. As Eisenman wrote in one of his early essays on Terragni—indicating his intent to use these strategies as prescriptive design tools—"while formal analysis is a valuable art-historical method, in itself it can become merely descriptive—an exercise in intellectual gymnastics."[13]

Not only was the history of form rewritten, but Eisenman would subject "form" itself to perpetual revision through an exhaustive sequence of operations: transformation, decomposition, grafting, scaling, rotation, inversion, superposition, shifting, folding, etc. And it is the catalogue of these procedures that becomes the subject matter of architecture, a disciplinary precondition to a diagrammatic approach. Through an extreme logic, Eisenman engaged in a critique both *through* and *of* calculation (or mathematics) in the alternate senses of both Rowe's ideal geometries and Christopher Alexander's "goodness of fit."

By 1970 Eisenman would distinguish the practices of Corbusier and Terragni (and, indirectly, Rowe's formalism from his own) by incorporating terminology from the structural linguistics of Noam Chomsky. While Corbusier's architecture remains committed to creating new meaning through iconography, through the *semantics* of the object, Eisenman claims that Terragni's work is concerned with revealing a *syntactics* of the architectural language. This shift represents a move away from a concern with the *perceptual-aesthetic* qualities of the object toward an attempt to mark the *conceptual relationships* that underlie and make possible any (and every) particular formal arrangement. Thus, Terragni's work is said to mark the relationship between "surface structure" and "deep structure" through transformational methods that Eisenman attempts to disclose via a series of axonometric diagrams and projections. It should be noted here that the axonometric technique (or parallel projection) was one of the historical avant-garde devices recuperated by this generation, especially Eisenman and Hejduk.[14] In contrast to the other dominant mode of three-dimensional drawing, the central projection or perspective of Renaissance humanism, the axonometric favors the autonomy of the object by conveying measurable or objective information over

15

Frankfurt Rebstockpark

the distortion created by a vanishing point oriented to the viewing subject. Where Rowe's analyses were undertaken separately in plan and elevation, the axonometric simultaneously renders plan, section, and elevation, thus again collapsing the vertical and horizontal—an act that has been noted earlier, for example, as one aspiration of Venturi's Billdingboard. Moreover, unlike Corbusier's "regulating lines"— geometric descriptions appended to their objects after construction—the three-dimensional device of the axonometric enables analysis and object to become congruent.

Through his axonometric diagrams, Eisenman argues that Terragni develops a conceptual ambiguity by superimposing two conceptions of space—additive/layered and subtractive/volumetric—neither of which is dominant, but each of which oscillates with the other indefinitely. The effect of this dual reading is not primarily aesthetic, but operates as an index of a deep structure: that is, it investigates and makes apparent the possibilities and limitations of the architectural language itself. Eisenman's attention to form, then, can be seen as a means to advance this transformational method as both an analytic and synthetic design tool. It is an attempt to fulfill the historical avant-garde program of a temporal and spatial movement or dislocation that precludes any static con-

templation of the high-art object. In this way, Eisenman's "drawing on modernism," the diagrammatic supplements of his American graffiti, places the architectural object under erasure and initiates the process of its disappearance.

Contemporaneously with the critical-historical work on Terragni, Eisenman was beginning a series of architectural projects that would develop many of the transformational strategies he was "finding" in his analysis of the modern canon. The serially numbered transformational diagrams for Houses I and II, like the retrospective diagrams created for Terragni's work, suggest that the "final" built structures are merely indexical signs that point to a larger process of which they are only a part. Not only is movement generated across the series of individual frames—for the whole process most resembles a cinematic operation with its montage of stills—but, given the nature of axonometric projection (exaggerated here by being rendered transparently or as a wire frame), there is also constant oscillation and reversible movement within each diagram: the observer is now inside, now outside; now under, now over. Recalling the new hybrid role of the architect-critic, this effect suggests the coincidence and complicity between "internal" formal condition and "external" construction of subjectivity. In addition to the transforma-

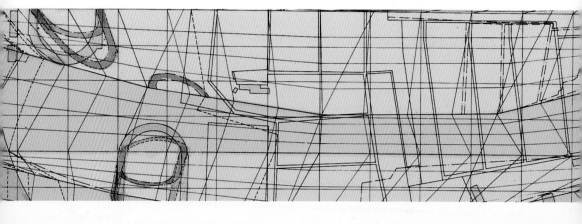

tional process effacing the object, this process also begins to displace the subject (as both designer and client) since the remaining architectural index is no longer dependent on the iconography or functions of man. This relates to Eisenman's argument that modern architecture was never sufficiently *modernist* due to its functionalism, that it amounted to nothing more than "a late phase of humanism."[15] Shifting architecture from a formal to a structuralist base, or from an iconic or semantic to an indexical or syntactic one, would enable architecture to finally register the insights of the modernist avant-gardes, an account which suspends classical-humanism's centrality of the subject and proposes architecture as "the abstract mediation between pre-existent sign systems,"[16] or, as he would write later of Corbusier's domino, as a "self-referential sign."

In displacing the author-subject (and, ultimately, the static object), Eisenman's early "cardboard" or "conceptual" architecture was designed "to shift the primary focus from the sensual aspects of objects to the universal aspects of object" and "to investigate the nature of what has been called formal universals which are inherent in any form of formal construct."[17] Eisenman's investigations thus required an initial ideal or generic form, which he often located in the cube, a neutral box that was typically (and somewhat less neutrally) designated as a nine-square. Unlike the initial premises of the nine-square problem as articulated in Austin (and as continued in Hejduk's private research into the theme through his seven Texas Houses from 1954–63), Eisenman does not privilege "space" (of the van Doesberg variety) as the dominant dynamic element to be read against the stasis of structure (of the Dom-ino type). Instead, in House II (1969), for example, multiple traces of column and wall systems are registered, traces which provide the overall spatial effects of the project. Thus, the activation of the structural grid or frame engenders the spatial event of the object—a kind of objectification of the structure, similar to Eisenman's association of architecture more with the *study* of language than with language itself. This tactic will reappear in the later work when there is a becoming-figure of the structure (see, for example, the Aronoff Center) or a mannerism of the grid which will finally manifest itself through the organization of the fold (e.g., Rebstockpark).

In House VI (1973–76), the classical nine-square organization initially deployed in the earlier houses comes to be seen as a more modernist four-square, an organization that will become more evident in the subsequent houses. Across the entire series of

17

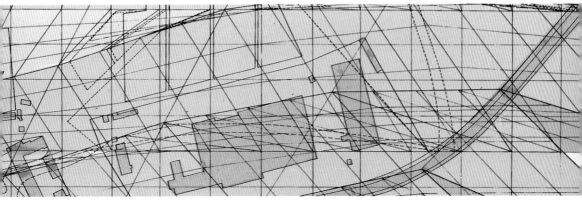

18

projects, however, Eisenman works within the strictures of the high modern diagram only to undo its fundamental principles and values, subverting the classical-humanist logic of the nine-square. In other words, Rowe's mannerist-modern conception of form as the relation of *space* and *structure* is now understood as the more provisional outcome of *time* and *movement*. In House VI specifically, the facades are no longer the primary vertical data for the reading of phenomenal transparencies, but are pushed to the interior such that the periphery now crosses at the center of the structure. Floating above the ground with no visible entry, it is a house which for all practical purposes could be upside down and inside out. Here, the value of frontality that had accompanied the flat, pictorial associations of plan and elevation in the writings and analyses of Rowe and Slutzky is undermined by the temporal and cinematic displacements provided by the axonometric. With Eisenman, the nine-square is no longer thought through the logic of painting, but through film, and it is this conception that enables it to exist as simultaneously experience and representation.

> House VI . . . exists as both an object and a kind of
> cinematic manifestation of the transformational
> process, with frames from the idea of a film being

independently perceptible within the house. Thus the object not only became the end result of its own generative history but retained this history, serving as a complete record of it, process and product beginning to become interchangeable.[18]

Described through serially arranged axonometric diagrams, Eisenman's houses are conceived as part of a cinematic movement, arbitrary stills translated into three dimensions from a potentially endless series.

Whether understood as a move from ambiguity to undecidability or from binary oppositions to micro-multiplicities, Eisenman's more recent work insists upon a surface reading that questions the possibility of the embodiment of meaning, and seems to operate only as an endless chain of conjunctions—*and, and, and* . . . one thing after the other. There is here a literal repetition (like that eschewed in Rowe's dismissal of the Bauhaus or in Michael Fried's rejection of minimalism) that wagers on the chance for an other condition to emerge through the machinic (in a broadly bio-mechanical sense) process of iteration. In fact, the projects that have been evolving since the Wexner Center cannot really be discussed as "works" or "objects" or "forms" or even "structures"—all these terms being too aesthetic or technical, too well demarcated and defined. Rather, they really seem to

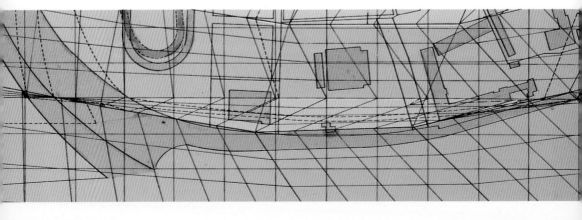

be just "things," with all the formless and transformative possibilities of the monstrous and grotesque that the term implies. These recent rhizome-worm "things" seem to frustrate and defeat formal analysis and indicate a transition from the clear structuralism of the early Roland Barthes to the base materialism of Georges Bataille, theorist of the excess. In his dictionary-like entry on the term *formless*, Bataille writes that "what it designates has no rights and gets itself squashed everywhere, like a spider or an earthworm."[19] In the post-vermiform projects since the Columbus Convention Center, the theoretical investigation of form has increasingly moved to an embrace of the *informe*, or a condition that Eisenman and his colleagues have referred to as "weak form."

For Eisenman, architecture—unlike writing—must struggle against its literal presence, which has traditionally been reinforced by the icons of "strong form." To articulate this non-dialectical condition between presence and absence, Eisenman posits the term "presentness" as one possibility for a "weak" practice, the hazard of architecture as event. While both he and Michael Fried are opposed to literal presence, Eisenman's use of the term must be distinguished from Fried's usage of the concept. For Fried, presentness implies a bounded object of depth and plenitude, the quality of which is instantaneously

self-evident such that it induces immediate faith and conviction. In this way, Eisenman's use has more in common with the perpetual reframing and temporal limitlessness of minimalist work that Fried was arguing against. In fact, minimalism operates precisely in a *diagrammatic* manner in that it solicits and undermines a key opposition of formalist modernism— namely, that between painting and sculpture—as it can be seen as emerging in response to developments in either medium (which, of course, would be impossible from the high modernist dicta of medium specificity and boundary maintenance). Finally, whereas Fried's "presentness" relies on a condition of timelessness, Eisenman's is involved with the state of "singularity"—i.e., a specific moment in a phase transition where diverse forces acting on matter induce the emergence of unforeseeable traits.

An early form of this singularity can be glimpsed in a project like the Rebstockpark proposal for the development of 200,000 square meters of offices and housing in Frankfurt (1991), an urban analog to the cinematic chronography of Alain Resnais and Robbe-Grillet's *Last Year at Marienbad*. Here, the between-condition of presentness requires a consideration of the arbitrary, the accidental. Rather than a narrative (strong-time) succession of presents (as, perhaps, represented in the Wexner Center), these

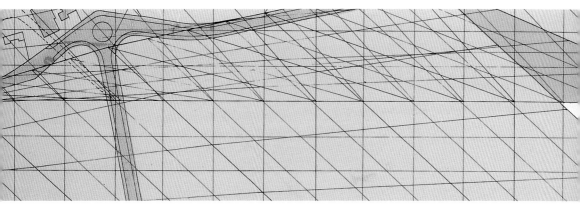

Frankfurt Rebstockpark

event-folds inhabit "peaks of present," where there is a coexistence of a present of the future, a present of the present, and a present of the past. In describing the time-image found in the work of Robbe-Grillet, Gilles Deleuze writes:

> An accident is about to happen, it happens, it has happened; but equally it is at the same time that it will take place, has already taken place and is in the process of taking place; so that, before taking place, it has not taken place, and, taking place, will not take place . . . etc.[20]

In the undecidability of whether the Rebstock site has contracted to absorb a neutral exterior net or is in the process of expanding to unfold its information across a larger area, the project offers an urban version of peeks at presentness, similar to the literary and cinematic visions of Robbe-Grillet and the mathematical models of Rene Thom. In both large- and small-scale episodes there is a multiplication of tenses: already folded, folding, not yet folded. Beginning with Rebstock—and continuing through the Church for the Year 2000, Bibliothèque de L'IHUEI, the Virtual House, and the IIT Campus Center—the "movement-image" of the earlier projects (where the diagram was limited to a linear unfolding of time, the recuperation of a genealogy for the work, such that time existed as a Muybridge-like dependent-variable of movement) has been displaced by a "time-image." Curiously, as intensified field conditions rather than distorted generics or ideals, these projects resemble more Rowe's denigrated diagram, "program without plan," than they do "plan without program."

In distinguishing "the event" from a narrative sequence organized by plot, John Rajchman maintains that it is "a moment of erosion, collapse, questioning, or problematization of the very assumptions of the setting within which a drama may take place, occasioning the chance or possibility of another, different setting."[21] Events are not in themselves accidental so much as the fact that their occurrence engenders the realization that what has been taken to be the necessary and natural is accidental. The Rebstock project directs an architectural "event," a manifestation of "weak time," to the extent that it elicits an active reframing of typology, context, function, and archaeology. Neither historicist nor progressive—and therefore other than the category of the possible—this kind of time can be thought of as "virtual," that which is merely an historical impossibility, not a logical or necessary one. As an investigation of the virtual, the Rebstock proposal performs an experimentation rather than an interpretation. And it is through this experimental quality—

presentness as the untimely or singular—that the scheme projects a "virtual reality." It is from this point that it might be possible to begin an evaluation of the fold in Eisenman's most recent work, for the fold is precisely a map of the event, a geometric description of the unexpected, *a diagram of the virtual.*

Certainly, in the trajectory from Venturi's Billdingboard to Eisenman's mannered manipulation of the axonometric evidenced in House X and Fin d'Ou T Hou S, the fold is perhaps the most advanced and economical device for collapsing vertical and horizontal, reversing inside and out. As an emblem for the hybrid activities of the architect-critics (and their privileged *métier* of paper), the fold is simply the shortest distance between two disciplines, two incommensurate discourses. As a figure, the fold immediately indexes a process, an activity. Unlike the secondary transformation or decomposition of an ideal or generic form such as the cube, a fold is at once a thing and its process. It is the *operation* of folding that generates the form, before which the thing simply did not exist. In this way the fold is not a mere *distortion of* or *opposition to* a clear formal type (e.g., as with the erosion of a cube), but evinces a repetition that produces something entirely new, an emergent organization that, in its most successful actualizations, is not simply dismissible as a "fallen" or debased ideal.

For Eisenman, then, the instrumentalization of the fold—translating this operational figure into a technique now made available to the repertoire of architectural production—resolved many of the dilemmas (and incompatibilities) internal to the two phases of his earlier work. In other words, while the house series developed through the manipulations of internal structure, the archaeological projects were engendered by the external contingencies of the contextual field. In addition to providing a means to negotiate the relations between the internal frame structure and the external urban grid, the fold enabled the development of figural effects (which had been precluded by the earlier house processes) as well as complex sections (which were hindered by the plan orientation of the larger scale archaeological work). Moreover, since the *informe* is not simply the negation of form, but a more complex maintenance and subversion of it, the fold allowed a relaxation of homogenous or hierarchical organizations without completely abandoning a geometric rigor or discipline. Given that the fold exists as one aspect of an alternative (or topological) mathematics, in this way, too, it promises to overcome not only the formalism of Rowe's classical mathematics but also a faith in the efficient functionality of Alexander's cybernetic version. In the movement from structuralist forms to

21

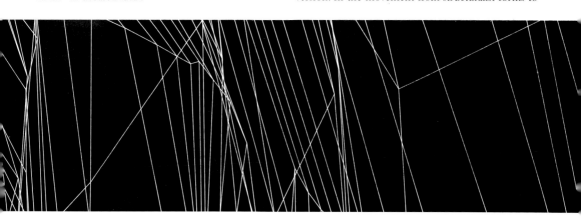

22

textual grafts to folded singularities, Eisenman has provided a coherent program for the dual project of dismantling the classical-modernist object and the liberal-humanist subject. While the house series focused on *process* as a way to displace the designer as an authoring agent, the archaeological projects (from Cannaregio to Wexner) sought new definitions of *context* that would destabilize the static identity of place. As a continuation of these reconfigurations of *process* and *context*, the folded projects have added a concern with *section* as a critique of the planimetric decidability of typology, which tends to contain objects through a limited logic of extrusion.

For the two decades following its introduction in 1957, the nine-square served as the discipline's formal introduction to itself, establishing the discourse on space and structure, and providing a series of solution sets through the allied design research of Hejduk, Eisenman, and others. In advanced academic and professional contexts after 1974, however, that epistemology of space was rapidly replaced by a pragmatics of force, such that the high modern diagram of the nine-square—which had served the formal purposes of the first generation's semiotic critique—came to be supplanted by a very different kind of diagram, a diagram that took its historical form in the discussions of "panopticism" by Michel Foucault

and Deleuze. For these thinkers, panopticism exists as *the* diagram of modern disciplinary societies, one which underlies multiple institutional types (prisons, hospitals, schools, factories, barracks, etc.), and one that can be most abstractly characterized by the attempt "to impose a particular conduct on a particular human multiplicity."[22] Not since Piranesi have prisons provided such an opportunity for extreme architectural speculation, and soon after Rem Koolhaas's "Exodus" project, he and his Office for Metropolitan Architecture (OMA) had the chance to engage directly the panoptic diagram in a design study for the renovation of Koepel Prison in Arnheim (1979–81), originally built according to Jeremy Bentham's principles in 1787. Rather than attempting to formalize any current (but soon to be obsolete) vision of prison management, OMA proposes in a sense to stage various diagrams of power:

> If prison architecture today can no longer pretend to embody an "ideal," it could regain credibility by introducing the theme of revision as raison d'être. A modern prison architecture would consist of a prospective archaeology, constantly projecting new layers of "civilization" on old systems of supervision. The sum of modifications would reflect the never-ending evolution of systems of discipline.[23]

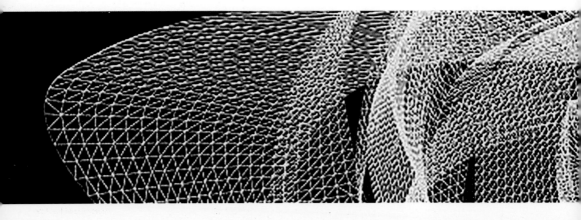

Thus, the importance of the lesson of panopticism is not simply to appropriate that figure as the new organizational system, but generally to understand (and configure) society as a plastic entity, susceptible to multiple (virtual) diagrams and possibilities for arrangement.

Having identified this connotative shift in the way in which the diagram has become instrumentalized in architecture over the last few decades, however, one should not mistake this transition for some essential opposition. Despite the posturing by several critics and architects alike, Koolhaas and Eisenman, for example, have much more in common with each other than either the former has with Jon Jerde or the latter has with Frank Gehry. Working diagrammatically—not to be confused with simply working with diagrams—implies a particular orientation, one which displays at once both a social *and* a disciplinary project. And it enacts this possibility not by representing a particular condition, but by subverting dominant oppositions and hierarchies currently constitutive of the discourse. Diagrammatic work, then (and this includes the projects of Eisenman and Koolhaas), cannot be accounted for by reapplying the conventional categories of formal or functional, critical or complicit. It operates as an alternative to earlier attempts to put "architecture" in quotation marks (the compensatory or affirmative sign

of postmodernism) or append a "kick me" sign to its back (the apparently critical gesture of early deconstructivism now institutionalized in a few Ph.D. programs throughout the country). Diagrammatic work is projective in that it opens new (or, more accurately, "virtual") territories for practice, in much the way that Deleuze describes the diagrammatic painting of Francis Bacon as overcoming the optical bias of abstract art as well as the manual gesturality of action painting:

> A Sahara, a rhinoceros skin, this is the diagram suddenly stretched out. It is like a *catastrophe* happening unexpectedly to the canvas, inside figurative or probabilistic data. It is like the emergence of another world. . . . The diagram is the possibility of fact—it is not the fact itself.[24]

This "emergence of another world" is precisely what the diagram diagrams. This begins to explain why, almost alone among those of their respective generations, both Eisenman and Koolhaas—teachers and critics as well as designers—persistently and curiously eschew *design* (and, along with it, that post-Renaissance trajectory of architecture obsessed with drawing, representation, and composition). This diagrammatic alternative can be seen initially in Eisenman's process automism and, more recently, in

23

Koolhaas's statistical research: complementary attempts to supplant design with the diagram, to deliver form without beauty and function without efficiency.

A diagrammatic practice (flowing around obstacles yet resisting nothing)—as opposed to the tectonic vision of architecture as the legible sign of construction (which is intended to resist its potential status as either commodity or cultural speculation)—multiplies signifying processes (technological as well as linguistic) within a plenum of matter, recognizing signs as complicit in the construction of specific social machines. The role of the architect in this model is dissipated, as he or she becomes an organizer and channeler of information, since rather than being limited to the decidedly vertical—the control and resistance of gravity, a calculation of statics and load—"forces" emerge as horizontal and nonspecific (economic, political, cultural, local, and global). And it is by means of the diagram that these new matters and activities—along with their diverse ecologies and multiplicities—can be made visible and related. Against some of the more currently naive extensions to the legacies of Eisenman and Koolhaas, it is thus important to avoid confining a diagrammatic approach to architecture as the expression of either presumed bio-mathematical imperatives or socio-economic inevitabilities, and understand architecture rather as a discursive-material field of cultural-political plasticity. To do otherwise would be to return to the inadequately diagrammatic options first outlined by Rowe (in terms of formal or analytical "truth") and Alexander (operational or synthetic "truth"). And it would also be to miss the virtual opportunities instigated by the design-research Eisenman has conducted for the last thirty years, simply (and brutally) collected here as a catalogue of procedures ("functions" or "tensors"), an architecture that has come to deviate from *a priori* geometry as well as from social accommodation in favor of Bacon's "possibilities of fact."

----

1. Christopher Alexander, *Notes on the Synthesis of Form* (Cambridge: Harvard University Press, 1964). For more on the "debate" between Eisenman and Alexander, see "Contrasting Concepts of Harmony in Architecture," *Lotus International* 40 (1983).

2. Reyner Banham, "A Black Box," in *A Critic Writes* (Berkeley: University of California Press, 1996), p. 298.

3. Colin Rowe, "Program versus Paradigm: Otherwise Casual Notes on the Pragmatic, the Typical, and the Possible," in *As I Was Saying*, vol. 2 (Cambridge: MIT Press, 1996), p. 10.

4. Later, this transformation will become more evident via architectural strategies of "folding," procedures that in part continue the complication of vertical and horizontal while exaggerating the dematerialization of "paper architecture."

5. This view of repetition follows from Gilles Deleuze's account of two ways to conceive difference: "Only that which is alike differs," and "Only differences are alike." In the first version difference can only derive from a prior autonomy or identity (e.g., the way a right and left

shoe are different by their relation to a prior identity, the pair), while in the second version differences operate horizontally rather than vertically, in a state of becoming identical (e.g., the surrealist encounter of the sewing machine and the umbrella). See *The Logic of Sense*, trans. Mark Lestor (New York: Columbia University Press, 1990) and *Difference and Repetition*, trans. Paul Patton (New York: Columbia University Press, 1994).

6. Gilles Deleuze, "Plato and the Simulacrum," *October* 27 (Winter 1983), p. 56.

7. Colin Rowe, "The Mathematics of the Ideal Villa," in *The Mathematics of the Ideal Villa and Other Essays* (Cambridge: MIT Press, 1976), pp. 15–16.

8. Colin Rowe, *Five Architects* (New York: Oxford University Press, 1975), p. 8.

9. Rowe, "The Mathematics of the Ideal Villa," p. 16.

10. For a detailed history of this program from an "insider," see Alexander Caragonne's *Texas Rangers: Notes from an Architectural Underground* (Cambridge: MIT Press, 1995).

11. This studio problem was paralleled in Hejduk's personal work with his seven "Texas Houses," a series begun in 1954 and later dedicated to Rowe and Robert Slutzky. See John Hejduk, *Mask of Medusa* (New York: Rizzoli, 1985), p. 197 and pp. 222–37.

12. Rowe, *Five Architects*, p. 7.

13. Peter Eisenman, "From Object to Relationship II: Giuseppe Terragni's Casa Giuliani Frigerio," *Perspecta* 13/14 (1971), p. 41.

14. While widely deployed by the modernist avant-gardes of the 1920s and 1930s, the axonometric projection virtually disappeared as a graphic tool until the late 1950s, being eschewed by those attempting to mimic more pictorial and static media in the postwar reconstruction of high modernism. Rowe and Johnson, for example, have explicitly come out against the effects of "floating," "rotation," and "the diagonal" associated with the isometric or axonometric. It will be suggested later that Eisenman does not recuperate the axonometric simply as a representational tool, but as a design tool, using its characteristics as a generative device. For a historical discussion of the axonometric, see Yve-Alain Bois, "El Lissitzky: Radical Reversibility," *Art in America* (April 1988), pp. 160–80, and "Metamorphosis of Axonometry," *Daidalos* 1 (1981), pp. 40–58, as

well as Robin Evans, "Architectural Projection," *Architecture and its Image*, eds. Eve Blau and Edward Kaufman (Montreal: Canadian Centre for Architecture, 1989), pp. 19–35.

15. Peter Eisenman, "Post-Functionalism," *Oppositions* 6 (Fall 1976), p. ii (unnumbered).

16. Eisenman, "Post-Functionalism," p. iii (unnumbered).

17. Peter Eisenman, "Notes on Conceptual Architecture," *Casabella* 359/360 (1971), p. 55. For an earlier though similar formulation, see "Towards an Understanding of Form in Architecture," *Architectural Design* (October 1963), pp. 457–58.

18. Peter Eisenman, "Misreading Peter Eisenman," *Houses of Cards* (New York: Oxford University Press, 1987), pp. 178 and 181. See also Peter Eisenman, "House VI," *Progressive Architecture* (June 1977), p. 59: "[T]he designs for House VI are symbiotic with its reality; the house is not an object in the traditional sense—that is the end result of a process—but more accurately a record of a process. The house, like the set of diagrammatic transformations on which its design is based, is a series of film stills composed in time and space." For more on the idea of architecture as document, see Venturi's similar discussion of the wall in *Complexity and Contradiction in Architecture*.

19. Georges Bataille, "Formless," in *Visions of Excess: Selected Writings, 1927–1939* (Minneapolis: University of Minnesota Press, 1985), p. 31.

20. Gilles Deleuze, *Cinema 2: The Time-Image* (Minneapolis: University of Minnesota Press, 1989), p. 100.

21. John Rajchman, *Philosophical Events: Essays of the '80s* (New York: Columbia University Press, 1991), p. viii.

22. Gilles Deleuze, *Foucault* (Minneapolis: University of Minnesota Press, 1988), p. 34. For Foucault's discussion, see *Discipline and Punish* (New York: Pantheon, 1977), originally published as *Surveiller et punir* (Paris: Gallimard, 1975), and "The Eye of Power," in *Power/Knowledge: Selected Interviews and Other Writings, 1972–1977*, ed. Colin Gordon (New York: Pantheon, 1980).

23. Rem Koolhaas, "Revision," in *S,M,L,XL* (New York: Monacelli Press, 1996), p. 241.

24. Gilles Deleuze, "The Diagram," in *The Deleuze Reader*, Constantin V. Boundas, ed. (New York: Columbia University Press, 1993), pp. 194, 199.

25

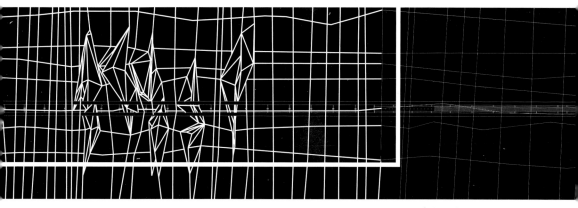

Diagram: An Original Scene of Writing

Peter Eisenman

As in all periods of supposed change, new icons are thrust forward as beacons of illumination. So it is with the idea of the diagram. While it can be argued that the diagram is as old as architecture itself, many see its initial emergence in Rudolf Wittkower's use of the nine-square grid in the late 1940s to describe Palladian villas. The diagram's pedigree continued to develop in the form of the nine-square problem as practiced in the American architectural academy of the late 1950s and early '60s, when it was seen as an antidote to the bubble diagramming of the Bauhaus functionalism rampant at Harvard in the late 1940s and to the *parti* of the French academy that was still in vogue at several East Coast schools well into the late 1960s. As a classical architectural diagram, the *parti* was embodied with a set of preexistent values such as symmetry, the *marche*, and *poché*, which constituted the bases of its organizing strategy. The bubble diagram attempted to erase all vestiges of an embodied academicism in the *parti*. In so doing, it also erased the abstract geometric content of the nine-square.

Generically, a diagram is a graphic shorthand. Though it is an ideogram, it is not necessarily an abstraction. It is a representation of something in that it is not the thing itself. In this sense, it cannot help but be embodied. It can never be free of value or meaning, even when it attempts to express relationships of formation and their processes. At the same time, a diagram is neither a structure nor an abstraction of structure. While it explains relationships in an architectural object, it is not isomorphic with it.

In architecture the diagram is historically understood in two ways: as an explanatory or analytical device and as a generative device. Although it is often argued that the diagram is a postrepresentational form, in instances of explanation and analysis the diagram is a form of representation. In an analytical role, the diagram represents in a different way from a sketch or a plan of a building. For example, a diagram attempts to uncover latent structures of organization, like the nine-square, even though it is not a conventional structure itself. As a generative device in a process of design, the diagram is also a form of representation. But unlike traditional forms of representation, the diagram as a generator is a mediation between a palpable object, a real building, and what can be called architecture's interiority. Clearly this generative role is different from the diagram in other discourses, such as in the parsing of a sentence or a mathematical or scientific equation, where the diagram may reveal latent structures but does not explain how those structures generate other sentences or equations. Similarly, in an architectural context, we must ask what the difference is between a diagram and a geometric scheme. In other words, when do nine squares become a diagram and thus more than mere geometry?

Wittkower's nine-square drawings of Palladio's projects are diagrams in that they help to explain Palladio's work, but they do not show *how* Palladio worked. Palladio and Serlio had geometric schema in mind, sometimes explicit and sometimes implicit, which they drew into their projects. The notations of dimensions on the Palladian plans do not correspond to the actual project but to the diagram that is never drawn. A diagram implicit in the work is often never made explicit. For example, as Kurt Forster has noted, in the earliest parchment drawings in architecture, a diagrammatic schema is often drawn or etched into the surface with a stylus without being inked. The later inking of the actual project over this then becomes a superposition of a diagrammatic trace. In many of these drawings—from late Gothic architecture to the Renaissance—the overlay does not actually take all of the diagrammatic imprint, only partial traces of it. The quality of the ink on the page changes where it runs over the diagram as opposed to the places where the diagram is actually part of the plan of the building. Thus, there is a history of an architecture of traces, of invisible lines and diagrams that only become visible through various means. These lines are the trace of an intermediary condition (that is, the diagram) that exists between what can be called the anteriority and the interiority of architecture; the summation of its history as well as the projects that could exist are indexed in the traces and the actual building.

The diagram is not only an explanation, as something that comes after, but it also acts as an intermediary in the process of generation of real space and time. As a generator there is not necessarily a one-to-one correspondence between the diagram and the resultant form. There are many instances, for example, in Le Corbusier's Modulor where the diagram is invisible in the building, yet it reappears as a repetitive element that occurs at many different scales, repeated in little segments of houses to large segments of urban plans, yet it is rarely an explicit form. Thus Le Corbusier's state-

ment that the plan is the generator will be seen to be different from the diagram is the generator. There are many examples of diagrams where a variety of shapes can be arrived at through a geometry that is exfoliated into different shapes. For example, Villard d'Honnecourt used geometric matrices to evolve natural and animal forms. One of the most interesting is the manifestation of a camel drawn from interlocking squares and diagonals. In the chateau architecture of the Loire Valley in the 16th century there are irregular forms that could only have been produced through some sort of manipulation of diagrammatic geometry into three-dimensional process called "stereotomy." Stones were cut from templates generated by these kinds of diagrams. As Kurt Forster notes, in the late Gothic, for example, there is a diagrammatic process that leads the schematic articulation of foliage on column capitals to change from a stylized or conventional nature with bilateral symmetries to a more naturalistic, free-form nature. Such a process differs from the straightforward manipulation of geometry that was the tradition in Gothic leaf capitals. The naturalistic evolution of these other capitals comes not from geometry but from a diagram. In this sense, the diagram becomes an intermediary condition between a regular base

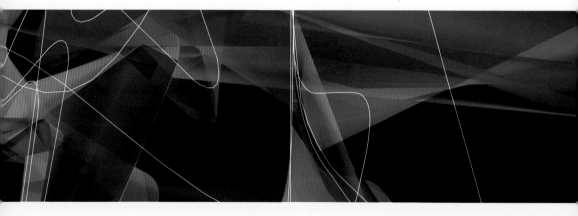

geometry and the capital itself. Here the diagram acts neither as geometry nor as the existent capital. It is a trace or phantom, which acts between something which can be called the interiority of architecture and the specific capital; between some explicit geometric formation which is then transformed by the diagram or intermediary process onto a result.

Reacting against an understanding of the diagram that characterized it is an apparently essentialist tool, a new generation, fueled by new computer techniques and a desire to escape its perceived Oedipal anxieties—with regard to the generation of their mentors—is today proposing a new theory of the diagram based partly on Gilles Deleuze's interpretation of Foucault's recasting of the diagram as "a series of machinic forces," and partly on their own cybernetic hallucinations. In their polemic, the diagram has become a keyword in the interpretation of the new. This question challenges both the traditional geometric bases of the diagram and the sedimented history of architecture, and in so doing they question any relation of the diagram to architecture's anteriority or interiority.

The second point Deleuze makes is that the diagram is different from structure. The classical architectural idea of a diagram exhibits a belief in structure as something that is hierarchical, static, and has a point of origin. Deleuze says that a diagram is a supple set of relationships between forces. It forms unstable physical systems that are in a perpetual disequilibrium. Deleuze says that diagrams that deal with distribution, serialization, and formalization are all structural mechanisms in that they lead to structure and a belief in structuring as an underlying principle of organization. If a structure is seen as a vertical or hierarchical ordering of its constituent parts, the diagram must be conceived both horizontally and vertically, both as a structure and something which resists structuring: "From one diagram to the next, new maps are drawn; thus there is no diagram that does not also include besides the points which it connects up (that is, besides its structural component) a certain relatively free or unbound points, points of creativity, change and resistance to that existing building." In this sense, diagrams are those forces which appear in every relation from one point to another, as superimposed maps. The distinction between Deleuze's idea of superimposition and my use of the term *superposition* is critical in this context. Superimposition refers to a vertical layering differentiating between ground and figure. Superposition refers to a coextensive, horizontal layering where

29

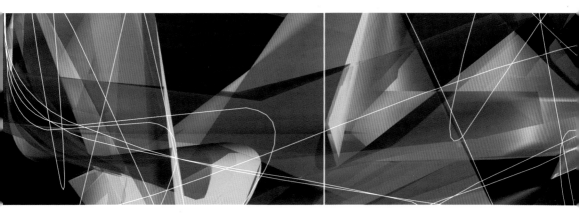

30

there is no stable ground or origin, where ground and figure fluctuate between one another.

Thus diagrams for Deleuze must have a non-structuring or informal dimension. It is "a functioning abstracted from any obstacle or friction, detached from any specific use." This is an important movement away from the classical idea of an architectural diagram. Deleuze says that "a diagram is no longer an auditory or visual archive, but a map, a cartography that is coextensive with the whole social field. It is an abstract machine." This abstract machine is defined by its functioning in unformed matter, as a series of processes that are neither mechanical nor organic. The diagram then is both form and matter, the visible and the articulable. Diagrams for Deleuze do not attempt to bridge the gap between these pairs, but rather attempt to widen it, to open the gap to other unformed matters and functions which will become formed. Diagrams, then, form visible matter and formalize articulable functions.

R.E. Somol follows Deleuze in situating these ideas of the diagram in architecture. For Somol, diagrams are any kind of explanatory abstraction: "cartoons, formulas, diagrams, machines, both abstract and concrete. Sometimes they are simply found and other times they are manipulated." A partial list of what Somol labels as "previous" diagrams includes the nine-square, the Panopticon, the Dom-ino, the skyscraper, the duck and the decorated shed, the fold, and bachelor machines. Somol says that he is searching for an alternative way of dealing with architecture's history, "one not founded on resemblance and return to origins but on modes of becoming an emergence of difference." The problem with this idea of the diagram as matter, as flows and forces, is that it is indifferent to the relationship between the diagram and architecture's interiority, and in particular to three conditions unique to architecture: (1) architecture's compliance with the metaphysics of presence; (2) the already motivated condition of the sign in architecture, and (3) the necessary relationship of architecture to a desiring subject.

Somol's argument for a diagrammatic project takes as axiomatic that every design project, whether in practice or in the university, needs to take up anew the issue of what constitutes the discipline or, in other words, that architecture both as a discipline and a social project needs to suspend and rearrange ruling oppositions and hierarchies currently in operation. This would suggest that design projects and processes cannot simply be derived from their contexts, but rather must *trans-*

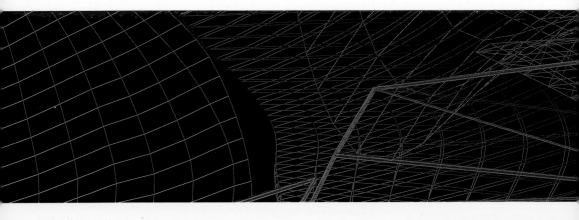

form their very social and intellectual contexts. In this sense, Somol's diagrammatic process, as a machinic environment, is already given as a social project. That is, it is not abstract or autonomous, but rather presumes that architecture already contains in its being (i.e., its interiority) the condition of the social.

If in the interiority of architecture there is a potentially autonomous condition that is not already socialized or that is not already historicized, one which can be distilled from a historicized and socialized interiority, then all diagrams do not necessarily take up new disciplinary and social issues. Rather, diagrams can be used to open up such an autonomy to understand its nature. If this autonomy can be defined as singular because of the relationship in architecture between sign and signified, and if singularity is also a repetition of difference, then there must be some existing condition of architecture in order for it to be repeated differently. This existing condition can be called architecture's interiority. When there is no interiority, that is, if there is no relationship between interiority and the diagram, there is no singularity which defines architecture.

If architecture's interiority can be said to exist as a singular rather than dialectical manifestation of a sign that contains its own signified, the motivation of the sign is already internalized and thus autonomous. Yet if the diagram is already social, as Somol suggests, this definition immediately historicizes autonomy. The notion of the diagram being proposed here attempts to overcome the historicization of the autonomy of architecture, that is, the already motivated nature of architecture's sign.

In this context, the relationship between the diagram and architecture's interiority is crucial. Foucault's understanding of an archive as the historical record of a culture, and of an archaeology as the scientific study of archival material, can be translated as architecture's anteriority and interiority. These cannot by their very nature be constituted merely by unformed matter, as Somol suggests, but in fact already contain presence, motivated signs, and a psychical desire for delineation by the subject of both ground and figure. A diagram of instability, of matter and flows, must find a way to accommodate these concerns specific to architecture. In this context, another idea of the diagram can be proposed, one which begins from Jacques Derrida's idea of writing as an opening of pure presence.

For Derrida, writing is initially a condition of repressed memory. The repression of writing is also the repression of that which threatens presence,

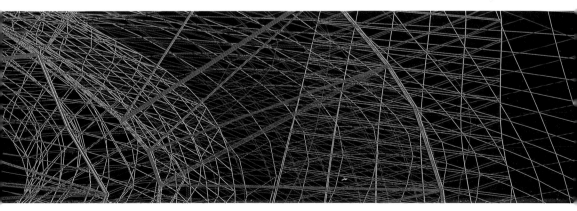

and since architecture is the *sine qua non* of the metaphysics of presence, anything that threatens presence would be presumed to be repressed in architecture's interiority. In this sense, architecture's anteriority and interiority can be seen as a sum of repressions. While all discourses, Derrida would argue, contain repressions that in turn contain an alternative interior representation, architecture must be seen as a special case because of its privileging of presence. If Derrida is correct, there is already given in the interiority of architecture a form of representation, perhaps as the becoming unmotivated of the architectural sign. This repressed form of representation is not only interior to architecture, but anterior to it. It is this representation in architecture that could also be called a writing. How this writing enters into the diagram becomes a critical issue for architecture.

One way that memory overcomes forgetting is through mnemonic devices. Written lists are a form of mnemonic device, but one that is graphic and literal; they do not represent or contain a trace. In architecture, literal notations can produce a plan but they have nothing to do with the diagram, because a plan is a literal mnemonic device. A plan is a finite condition of writing, but the traces of writing suggest many different plans. It is the idea of the

trace that is important for any concept of the diagram, because unlike a plan, traces are neither fully structural presences nor motivated signs. Rather, traces suggest potential relationships, which may both generate and emerge from previously repressed or unarticulated figures. But traces in themselves are not generative, transformative, or even critical. A diagrammatic mechanism is needed that will allow for both preservation and erasure and that can simultaneously open up repression to the possibility of generating alternative architectural figures which contain these traces.

Derrida says, "We need a single apparatus that contains a double system, a perpetually available innocence and an infinite reserve of traces." A diagram in architecture can also be seen as a double system that operates as a writing both from the anteriority and the interiority of architecture as well as from the requirements of a specific project. The diagram acts like a surface that receives inscriptions from the memory of that which does not yet exist—that is, of the potential architectural object. This provides traces of function, enclosure, meaning, and site from the specific conditions. These traces interact with traces from the interiority and the anteriority to form a superposition of traces. This superposition provides a means for

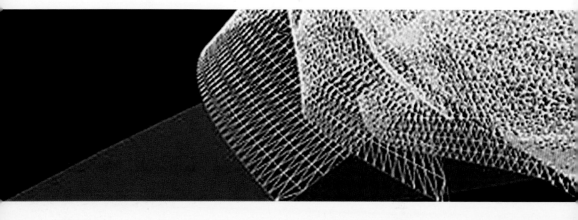

looking at a specific project that is neither condemned to the literal history of the anteriority of architecture, nor limited by facts, the reality of the particular site, program, context, or meaning of the project itself. Both the specific project and its interiority can be written onto the surface of a diagram that has the infinite possibility of inscribing impermanent marks and permanent traces. Without these permanent traces there is no possibility of writing in the architectural object itself.

If architecture's interiority is seen as already-written, then Derrida's use of Freud's double-sided Mystic Writing Pad could be one model for describing a conception of a diagram different from both the traditional one in classical architecture and the one proposed by Somol. Neither of these consider in any detail architecture's problem with the metaphysics of presence, the unmotivating of the sign, or the psychical problem of repression in both the interiority of architecture and in the subject. The analogy of the Mystic Writing Pad is useful because the specific conditions of site and the anteriority of architecture both constitute a form of psychical repression.

The Mystic Writing Pad, as proposed in Freud's analogy, consists of three layers: the outer layer or surface where the original writing takes place, a middle layer on which the writing is transcribed, and underneath, a tablet of impressionable material. Using a stylus, one writes on the top surface. Because of the surface underneath, the top surface reveals a series of black lines. When the top surface is lifted from the other two, the black lines disappear. What remains is the inscription on the bottom surface, the trace of the lines that have been drawn. The indentations made by the stylus remain, always present. Thus there are infinite possibilities for writing and rewriting on the top surface and a means of recording the traces of this writing as a series of superpositions on the tablet underneath. This recalls the traces of the earliest incisions on parchment that already exist in the anteriority of architecture as described above.

The architectural diagram, like the Mystic Writing Pad, can be conceived of as a series of surfaces or layers which are both constantly regenerated and at the same time capable of retaining multiple series of traces. Thus, what would be seen in an architectural object is both the first perceptual stimulus, the object itself, along with its aesthetic and iconic qualities, and another layer, the trace, a written index that would supplement this perception. Such a trace would be understood to exist before perception, in other words, before a perception is conscious of itself.

33

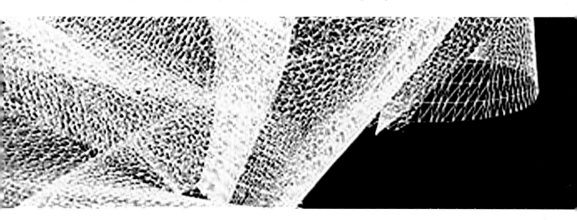

Derrida says, "Memory or writing is the opening of that process of appearance itself. The 'perceived' may only be read in the past, beneath perception and after it." The diagram understood as a strata of superposed traces offers the possibility of opening up the visible to the articulable, to what is within the visible. In this context, architecture becomes more than that which is seen or which is present; it is no longer entirely a representation or an illustration of presence. Rather, architecture can be a re-presentation of this intervening apparatus called the diagram. In this sense, the diagram could be understood to exist before the anteriority and the interiority of architecture. It exists as the potential space of writing, a writing which supplements the idea of an interiority before perception. This idea of an interiority as containing a palimpsest of an already-written undercuts the premise of architecture's origin in presence.

But there is also a temporality involved in the processes of the diagram. Derrida says that the Mystic Pad includes in its structure what Kant describes as the three modes of time: permanence, succession, and simultaneity. The diagram, like the writing pad, contains the simultaneity of the appearance on its surface, what would be akin to the black lines on the top layer of the pad, as well as the indentations in the wax below: the second aspect of the time of the diagram is succession, which is akin to the lifting up of the pad and is involved in erasure and the posting of a new image. This is the permanence in the wax itself. The diagram presents in such a context a discontinuous conception of time as the periodicity and the spacing of writing. These three conditions of time are not linear or connected in a narrative way. Thus, the diagram is an intermediate or interstitial condition which lies between in space and time— between the architectural object and the interiority of architecture.

Writing implies that in an architectural object, the object's presence would already contain a repetition. In this sense an architectural object would no longer be merely a condition of being, but a condition which has within itself both a repetition of its being and a representation of that repetition. If the interiority of architecture is singular as opposed to dialectical, and if that singularity can be defined as a repetition of difference, then architecture's interiority may be already written.

There is a second concern that the diagram must address, and that is the potential for the becoming unmotivated of the sign. The already-written introduces the idea of the index into the

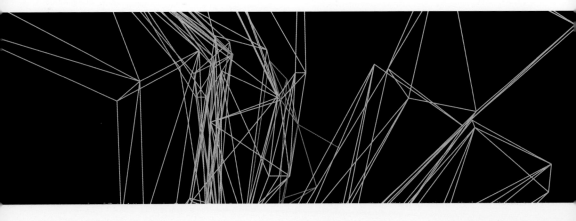

architectural object. The index is the first move-ment away from a motivated sign. Here, another layer must be added to the strata of the diagram, one which, through a process of blurring, finds new possibilities for the figural within architec-ture's interiority that could not have come from that interiority. An external condition is required in the process, something that will introduce a generative or transformative agent as a final layer in the diagrammatic strata. This external agent is not the expression of a desiring subject, but rather must come from outside of architecture as some previously unfigured, yet immanent agent in either the specific site, the program, or the history. It could take the form of a transparent pattern or screen, which causes the already imprinted to appear as other figurations, both blurring and revealing what already exists. This is similar to the action of a moiré pattern or filter, which permits these external traces to be seen free of their former architectural contexts.

The diagram acts as an agency which focuses the relationship between an authorial subject, an architectural object, and a receiving subject; it is the strata that exist between them. Derrida says that "Freud, evoking his representation of the psy-chical apparatus, had the impression of being faced with a machine which would soon run by itself. But what was to run by itself was not a mechanical re-presentation or its imitation but the psyche itself." The diagrammatic process will never run without some psychical input from a subject. The diagram cannot "reproduce" from within these psychical conditions. The diagram does not gener-ate in and of itself. It opens up the repression that limits a generative and transformative capacity, a repression that is constituted in both the anteriori-ty of architecture and in the subject. The diagram does not in itself contain a process of overcoming repression. Rather, the diagram enables an author to overcome and access the history of the discourse while simultaneously overcoming his or her own psychical resistance to such an act. Here, the dia-gram takes on the distancing of the subject-author. It becomes both rational and mystical, a strange superposition of the two. Yet according to Freud, only the subject is able to reconstitute the past; the diagram does not do this. He says, "There must come a time when the analogy between this appa-ratus and the prototype will cease to apply. This is true that once writing has been erased the Mystic Pad cannot 'reproduce' it from within; it could be a Mystic Pad indeed if, like our memory, it could accomplish that."

35

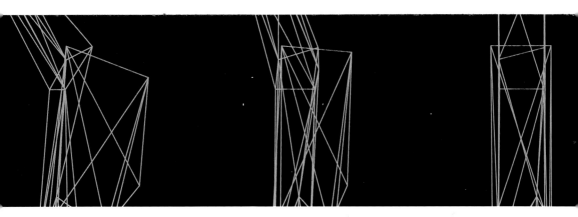

Diagrams of Anteriority

Peter Eisenman

Architecture is traditionally concerned with external phenomena: politics, social conditions, cultural values, and the like. Rarely has it theoretically examined its own discourse, its interiority. My work on the diagram is one such examination. It concerns the possibility that architecture can manifest *itself*, manifest its own interiority in a realized building. The diagram is part of a process that intends to open architecture to its own discourse, to its own rhetoric and thus to potential tropes which are latent within it. These tropes are not absolute. They are always relative to and contingent upon the historical conditions of any time. For example, the tropes and thus the rhetoric of architecture in the age of information is bound to be different from the meaning of architecture in the time of the industrial revolution. In themselves, these moments in time are not stable; they are constantly evolving and changing. This instability also affects architecture's interiority. Interiority in one sense conditions the way functions, sites, structures, aesthetics, politics, and social phenomena can be more corporeal, and how, in turn, that corporeality alters those particular social conditions. In other words, while the zeitgeist, i.e., the spirit of any age, causes changes in architecture, architecture in order to act critically must transgress and displace that very same spirit. While it is possible that architecture can manifest the political, social, aesthetic, and cultural conditions of any time, it will be argued here that through the agency of the diagram, which is a manifestation of architecture's interiority, architecture has the possibility of not merely representing but transforming and being critical of these socio-political conditions.

In the interiority of architecture there is also an *a priori* history, the accumulated knowledge of all previous architectures. This history can be called architecture's anteriority. It is the accumulation of the tropes and rhetoric used at different periods of time to give meaning to architecture's discourse. Today, for example, a computer program has no knowledge of this history; it can only produce illustrations of conditions that look architectonic. Yet if these anterior conditions of architecture are not part of any process of design, there can be no criticality, since there can be no commentary on the existing rhetoric. Criticality evolves out of the possibility of both repetition, to know what has gone before, and difference, to be able to change that history. Modeling blobs on the computer or random shapes by hand is flawed in that it does not take into account this anteriority. What these methods produce is a form of individual expression which on occasion has power to move, to motivate, and even to be critical, but which is a *unique* rather than a *singular* expression. Individual expression may always be different but it involves no repetition.

The singular is unlike individual or unique expression in the sense that it involves repetition and thus anteriority. A repetition implies something to be repeated—here, the anteriority of architecture—but this repetition, in order to be critical, is a repetition of difference rather than the repetition of the same. The singular causes architecture to be always in the present but different from its manifestation in the past. This past is the anteriority as it is manifest in the interiority of architecture.

In order for architecture's singularity, as a repetition of difference, to be of value, it has to be active in a design process. And in turn, such a design process must produce built objects which present this process of relating interiority and anteriority to the present at the same time that it makes that relationship manifest. That is, in addition to a program of functions, structure, enclosure, and site, the condition of architecture's interiority must somehow be able to be read in the physical object. The diagram is one potential means to articulate architecture's interiority, its sign and its being as a singular characteristic of architecture. A diagram is not a plan, nor is it a static entity. Rather it is conceived of as a series of energies which draw upon the interiority and anteriority of architecture as a potential for generating new configurations.

The diagram itself has a long history in architecture. While it is possible to trace such a history, what is more relevant in this context is to trace its evolution as a process of making manifest the interiority and anteriority of architecture. The evolution of the diagram in my work is such a process. The particular invocation of this process has given my work its signature, and, in a sense, the articulation of that signature is the diagrammatic process.

For Vitruvius, the signature process was the recording of fact. In the first century A.D., Vitruvius wrote his categorical treatise *The Ten Books on Architecture*. It was the first coherent compendium, in a way, of what architecture was and should be. Then, for over a thousand years, the architect disappeared. The Gothic cathedrals were built by master masons who had no plans and worked from chalk lines on the floor. They piled stone upon stone until the Gothic cathedrals became so high, as in Beauvais, that they fell down and were never completed.

It was not possible to have architects, per se, in the building campaigns that characterized these Gothic cathedrals because these campaigns lasted for centuries. The cathedrals began in one style, in one century, and were finished sometimes three centuries

later in an entirely different style. Also, as theocentric belief began to erode, the need arose to explain each discourse in terms of a new subject and a new object. Each discourse, from mathematics to physics, painting and sculpture, invented its own history, its own propelling mechanism, a new historicity that moved it from some point in the past to its then current place in the thirteenth, fourteenth, or fifteenth centuries. These histories needed to be developed in order to explain the subject, one newly evolved out of a theocentric view of the world into an anthropocentric one, and the object world that surrounded him. The subject needed answers to a new consciousness that could no longer be explained through divine revelation.

Out of this need, the subject-architect reemerged in the fifteenth century. Alberti's treatise *Della Pittura* (1436) developed for painting a history, and his *De Re Aedificatoria* (c. 1450) did the same for architecture. *De Re Aedificatoria*, while modeled after Vitruvius's treatise, is actually a critique of Vitruvius's ten books. Vitruvius's treatise is a series of value judgments about what should be and what ought to be. While Vitruvius said that a building should be commodious, firm, and delightful, Alberti implies that this is not what Vitruvius meant. Alberti suggests that Vitruvius did not mean that buildings should *be* structural, but that

38

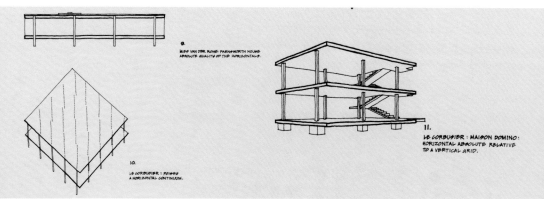

9.
MIES VAN DER ROHE: FARNSWORTH HOUSE.
ABSOLUTE QUALITY OF THE HORIZONTALS.

10.
LE CORBUSIER: POISSY.
A HORIZONTAL CONTINUUM.

11.
LE CORBUSIER: MAISON DOMINO:
HORIZONTAL ABSOLUTE RELATIVE
TO A VERTICAL GRID.

they should *look like* they are structural. It is clear that all buildings need to be structural, because if they are not structural, they do not stand up; they are not buildings. Now "look like they are structural" means that they should not only *be*, but that they should *represent* their being. With Alberti, architecture for the first time concerns not only its being—the facture itself—but also its representation both inside and outside of its being.

This condition of "look like" is a critical issue in the anteriority of architecture. Structural parameters gradually evolved out of Greek, Roman, and Gothic architecture, so that what was perceived as structural had to look structural to the eye of the beholder as the subject came into consciousness in the fifteenth century. This need introduced an idea of looking-in-the-present. This produced a condition in representation, an expectancy, which can be called *normal*. The idea of the normal does not occur in Alberti but rather later with Claude Perrault and Guarini, who said that the structural is what appears in the eye of the beholder to be structural.

The introduction of perspective also changed the parameters of representation. This implicated an active relationship between the human subject, again the eye of the beholder, and the object, into the interiority of architecture. Alberti introduced an idea of anteriority

as the necessary history of the discourse while Brunelleschi introduced an exteriority from mathematics and physics in the form of perspective. Since that time, the dominance of vision and the visible in the form of perspective has become so sedimented in architecture that it is assumed to be a natural condition. Such conditions as perspective and the like are continually sedimented into the interiority of architecture. The sedimentation of the visible is only one of many conventions that the diagram questions and attempts to displace.

Thus the first condition of architecture's manifestation of something other than its being is the representation of this being in the visible. This ultimately affects the idea of the diagram. For example, two of Brunelleschi's churches—San Lorenzo and Santo Spirito—show how the interiority of a discourse can be represented and manifested in a building as other than mere structure. In both cases, Brunelleschi uses Gothic structure in conjunction with perspectival vision to change their spatial conditions. In San Lorenzo, the first of the two churches, the three aisles converge perspectivally from a static viewpoint to create the notion and illusion of depth. While there is real depth, there is also the representation of depth. In Santo Spirito, again a three-aisle church with a Gothic structural organization, there is a representation of

39

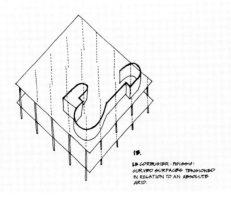

15.
LE CORBUSIER : POISSY:
CURVED SURFACES TENSIONED
IN RELATION TO AN ABSOLUTE
GRID.

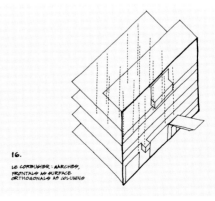

16.
LE CORBUSIER : AARCHES,
FRONTALS AS SURFACE
ORTHOGONALS AS COLUMNS

space as flat, giving a sense of layered picture planes. Many diagrams have been made of these spatial differences which give these phenomena a certain focus. However, the diagram is not a scientific instrument that gives a precise reading; rather it allows a given range of readings at the same time that it obscures others. The diagram can clarify the difference between San Lorenzo and Santo Spirito by focusing on, for example, their differing conditions of the subject: one requires a static subject looking at space through a conic vision from a single point of view, while the second requires a moving subject that sees the space as he or she continually progresses in and around it.

Such diagrams also contain in these manifestations of fifteenth-century perspectival vision a belief in the capacity to represent vision. Such a vision is assumed to have a structure that underlies the possibility of understanding space and time, and therefore also contains a belief in structure. Current post-structuralist thought questions both vision and structure, and thus the diagram also questions the sedimented anteriority of vision at the same time that it invokes it.

Prior to 1968, such a questioning would not have been directed toward these categories. Most critical manifestations of postwar thought were considered to be structural. Since 1968, structures are seen to contain their own repressive instruments. Thus there must

be an understanding of the nature of belief systems, the ideologies that inhabit these so-called rational or scientific diagrams as early as those of Brunelleschi, Alberti, or Leonardo da Vinci. These diagrams are in fact not neutral analytic devices but rather are occupied by their own belief systems. In this sense, anteriority as it evolves is also a manifestation of different belief systems, as well as a critique of those systems.

For example, Palladio introduces an idea of representation different from Brunelleschi and Alberti. Palladio, a stonemason by trade with no formal education, went to Rome early in his career to measure Roman ruins. Bramante freed Palladio and others to make a critical reading of these ruins, which then evolved into an entirely new type—the villa—in Palladio's work. The villa type of *en suite* as opposed to striated spatial organizations became the model for English country houses as well as American country houses, through the eighteenth century. The difference between these two types becomes important in the context of Palladio's drawings.

Palladio redrew all of his buildings in 1578, when he was seventy years old, for his famous *Four Books of Architecture*. They were redrawn as Palladio had conceptualized them. These drawings documented fragments of buildings from imperial Rome that he had originally sketched but then placed in a different con-

40

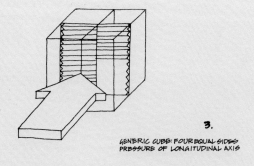

3.

GENERIC CUBE: FOUR EQUAL SIDES
PRESSURE OF LONGITUDINAL AXIS

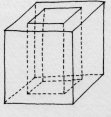

4.

HOLLOWING OUT OF CENTROIDAL
FORM TO PROVIDE FOR PROGRAMMATIC
REQUIREMENTS

text. Rather than a copy, their anteriority became part of this new villa type. This type also evolved from the Greek temple front, which Alberti had used in San Andrea in Mantua and which by that time was a vernacular icon, drained of its religious symbolism. Palladio took this architectural integer and deployed it in villa facades in many ways: in porticos that were projected from the volume of the building, on the volume of the building, and into the volume of the building. He also evolved variations on a series of elements taken from vernacular building in the Veneto, such as the location of chimneys and blank central panels, which would later appear in Le Corbusier's early work. Palladio fused giant orders with small orders, clashing different scales with one another, creating displacing relationships to what was then normalized. These transgressions of the normal produced critical conditions with respect to the then present. However, when these displacements become sedimented and thus normalized, they become part of the anteriority of architecture, and thus lose their criticality. It is the agency of the diagram which attempts to displace this sedimentation, and thus to open anteriority to its potential criticality.

The representations in Palladio's books were not about how one lived in the sixteenth century in the Venetian countryside; they were marks of a new manner of thinking about form and space in relationship to the human subject. For example, there were no corridors in Palladio's *en suite* villa type. All openings were related through rooms. Sometimes the interior relationships related to the exterior, and sometimes they did not. This disjunction between the interior relationships of rooms and doors to the facades was another displacement of the then normalized interiority of architecture. His drawings are not so much plans and elevations of real buildings as they are abstractions of those buildings, some of which were built, some of which were not. Palladio even called these drawings *inventions*. These drawings were involved in the beginning of architectural representation as something other than the marking of the fact itself, or the marking of the representation of the fact. In a sense, these early drawings of Palladio can be called second-degree representations: the first-degree representation being the plans and sections of the artifact itself. Most examples of second-degree representations could be considered diagrammatic in that they are not representations such as copies or models, but rather involve a certain level of criticality, a removal from the facts of the object. While type moves towards abstraction, it does so in a way that reduces the model, the copy, or the original. The diagram, on the other hand, contains more than the model. The type and the diagram are two

41

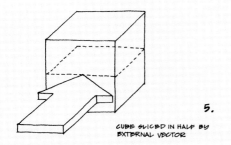

5.
CUBE SLICED IN HALF BY
EXTERNAL VECTOR

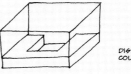

6.
DISLOCATION OF
COURT TO REAR.

different conditions of abstraction: type, the abstraction of a reduction to a normalization, and diagram, the abstraction that may generate into something more than the thing itself, and thus potentially overcome normalization.

This brings the issue of *presentness* into the question of representation and the diagram. Presentness is that condition which allows the object to remain unabsorbed into the normalized interiority of architecture. It allows the object to remain outside of its original time as a critical instrument. It is this level of criticality in presentness which inhabits the diagram as a second degree of representation. The diagrams that are inherent in Palladio do not exist in the many copies or models that followed, but only in their own condition of presentness, unabsorbed into a condition of what the eye expects to see. Palladio, in his criticality and transgression of the normal, will always potentially remain outside of what the eye allows the subject to absorb into a supposed normal vision of architecture. In this sense, Palladio's work is critical of vision.

In the intervening years between Palladio and early modernism, theories of architecture were written and rewritten as categorical treatises that laid out the essences and rules for an architecture whose interiority was assumed to be known and thus was conceived of as normal. After the French Revolution, these treatises became increasingly concerned with type because the revolution provoked the need to typify new institutions and make symbolic the prison, the library, the factory, or the clinic. They became symbols of the new revolutionary orders of society, creating the need to organize these expanding architectural functions. Books were produced codifying typical structures for these new uses. One was J.N.L. Durand's *Recueil et Parallèle des Édifices en Tout Genre*, which outlines the new functions of architecture as they could be defined in their many type variations. These publications reflected a need both to normalize and typify these new functions in order to provide some way of relating the past anteriority to the then present interiority.

The new building functions changed the way rooms related to one another; the Palladian villa gave way to what is called a *servant and served* relationship. The corridor became an instrument differentiating between the public and the private; the individual subject became a collective subject. When type moved from normalized type-structure in Durand to the French Beaux-Arts academy, it became what is known as a *parti*. A parti is a particular form of type. The parti adds to the type an architectural drapery; it was a way of relating building types to the individual under-

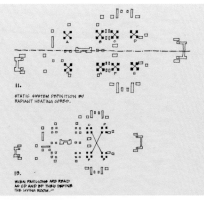

11.
STATIC SYSTEM DEFINITION BY
RADIANT HEATING CORES.

13.
WHEN PAVILIONS ARE READ
AS CD AND BF THEY DEFINE
THE LIVING ROOM.—

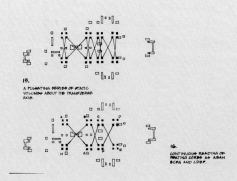

15.
A PULSATING SERIES OF STATIC
VOLUMES ABOUT THE TRANSVERSE
AXIS.

16.
CONTINUOUS READING OF
HEATING CORES AS ABAH
BCFA AND CDBF.

standing of the experience and use of a building. The Beaux-Arts parti was the reigning condition of anteriority from the middle of the nineteenth century well into the middle of the twentieth century. As late as 1968, in many schools of architecture in the United States, the parti as opposed to type or diagram was still in vogue. There were certain partis that were acceptable within the canon of type. For example, a parti said that it was impossible to place a column in the center of an opening, on the central axis of a building. There were certain rules and regulations for parti organizations: where one entered, how one entered, the relationship of the center to the edge, the relationship of the front to the back. All of these were proposed in yet more rule structures that pervaded architecture in both the English and French languages until the middle of this century.

In an attempt to overcome the academicism of the parti, Walter Gropius and others from the Bauhaus introduced the bubble diagram into the American architectural discourse. The bubble diagram, which was in reality a pictograph of functions had also a more subtle intention—to undermine the presence of anteriority in the building of the present. It is ironic that four hundred years after the fact, the bubble diagram joined with the idea of presentness in Palladio to attempt to subdue anteriority. But some-

thing was amiss. The bubble diagram was in reality a zeitgeist instrument, so in its denial of anteriority, it was not acting critically, but rather represented an attempt to normalize the present as a denial of any past. In this sense, the bubble diagram was also a denial of interiority.

Both the zeitgeist, as one form of a normalizing condition, and architecture's anteriority continually attempt to subdue the displacements of the diagram—that is, the transgressions of the present—into some kind of normalized interiority. One of the pitfalls of modern architecture was that it attempted to *express* the zeitgeist in its being rather than displacing it. Ultimately, modern architecture was absorbed by global capital, precisely because the ideology of modernism became normal and generic rather than critical. For it was that very same criticality of modern architecture that had set out fifty years earlier to deny the potential of global capital. The ideology of modernism, which was initially Marxist, became the vehicle for the absorption of Marxist ideology into global capital. The possibility of such a global capital today is a manifestation of the failure of modernism to transgress and displace its own space. In its attempt to manifest that zeitgeist, modern architecture lost the possibility for displacement and presentness, and thus its capacity to be diagrammatic.

43

12.
DEFINITION TO DOMINANT
CENTRAL AXIS WHEN READ AS
RC AND FR

14.
—WHEN READ AS AB–AH THEN
DEFINE THE RECEPTION HALL—
KITCHEN VOLUME .

17.
IT IS FURTHER POSSIBLE
TO READ DCBA AS A
UNITY.

Diagrams of Interiority
Peter Eisenman

Interiority: Grids

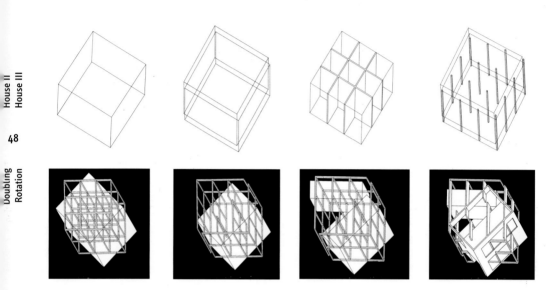

The use of diagrams in my work first appeared in my Ph.D. thesis in 1963. The diagrams evolved in response to Rudolf Wittkower's analysis of Palladian villas and Colin Rowe's further development of this form of analytical discourse in his comparisons of Le Corbusier and Palladio. While Wittkower's and Rowe's diagrams essentially relied on an analysis of the formal as a stable and *a priori* condition, my diagrams contained the seeds of something else: they proposed the possible opening up of the formal interiority of architecture to concerns of the conceptual, the critical and perhaps to a diagramming of a pre-existent instability in this interiority. This concern has occupied much of the work that has followed. While it was clear to me at the time that there was a difference between the diagrams of Rowe and Wittkower and those of their predecessors Heinrich Wölfflin and Paul Frankl, as well as other contemporary diagrams such as the Bauhaus bubble diagrams, I was not as conscious of the

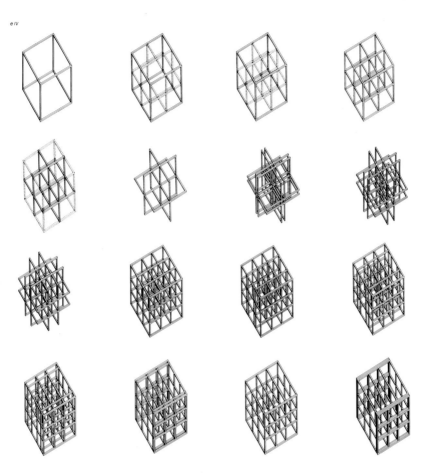

e IV

very real difference between my work and Rowe's as I am today.

Clearly, Rowe and Wittkower were involved in what could be called the articulation of formal principles in architecture; their work is a starting point for my use of the diagram in a re-examination of the formal. In this context, function, traditional aesthetics, social concerns, and metaphors of machines were for me always pallid justifications for a do-what-you-want expressionism. My use of the dia-

gram proposed a different rationale, one that could be both more logical and more involved with a process of architecture somewhat distant from the design process of the traditional author-architect. Such a logic could not be found in form itself, but rather in a diagrammatic process that had the potential to open up the difference between the form/content relationship in architecture and other disciplines, particularly the other plastic disciplines of painting and sculpture. While diagrams of

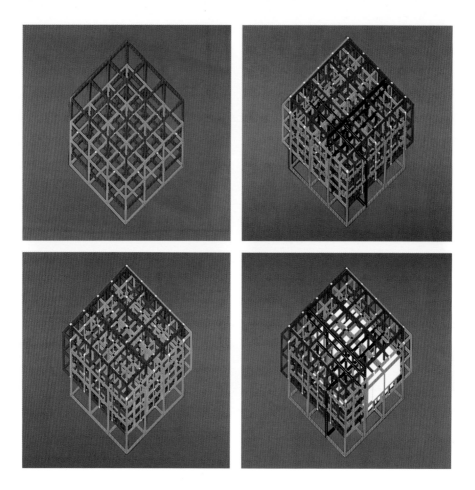

painting, sculpture, and architecture were often seen as similar in their content, my use of the diagram proposed that there was some critical difference between them. This difference was found in the unique relationship in architecture between its instrumentality and its iconicity, between architecture's function and its meaning, and ultimately between its sign and its signified. This was the foundation for my work on what was to be defined as architecture's singular interiority.

While Jacques Derrida would argue for the free play of linguistic signs, he rarely linked the sign's physical attributes to its sign value. Previously, specific forms in architecture were always linked to a function (a column must always have a shape and a material dimension) and, therefore, to a meaning. My initial idea in the use of the diagram was that the substrate of form, here referred to as an aspect of architecture's interiority, could be detached from such programmatic concerns. This is what Yve-Alain

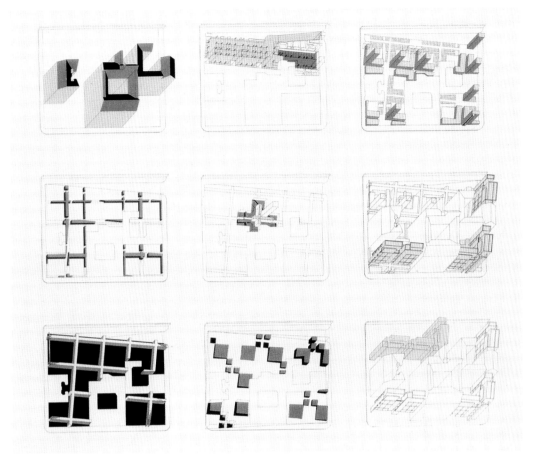

Bois and Rosalind Krauss have called the need to preserve the singularity of objects by cutting them off from their previous modes of legitimation. For architecture, this would mean a process that would displace form from its assumed necessary relationships to function, meaning, and aesthetics without at the same time necessarily denying the presence of these conditions. This act of displacement would become critical in the development of a diagrammatic process articulated in my Ph.D. thesis and later developed in my work on Giuseppe Terragni. It was also different from Wittkower's and Rowe's understanding of the formal.

Essentially, then, in my thesis I used the diagram to define the idea of the formal in two ways. First, and most obvious, the formal was distinguished from the aesthetic. Second, and a far more subtle concern, was that the formal was seen to be different from a stable set of forms in architecture's interiority. At the time this difference in the formal, particularly in rela-

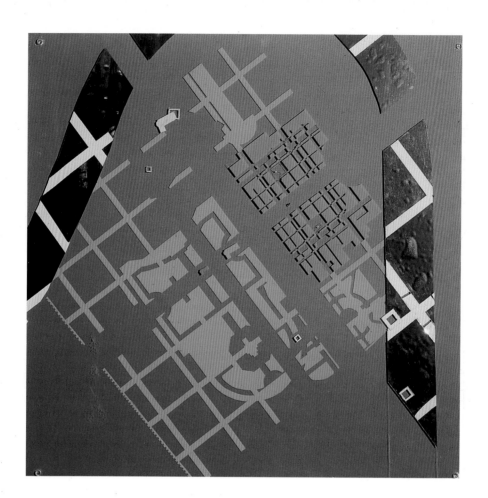

tion to the Modern Movement, remained nascent in the writing of my thesis. The nature of this difference was something that the diagram, as it was used in the thesis, presumed to explore.

My idea of the formal differed from an essentialist view of form, implied by Wölfflin and others, in that it articulated both a quality of what at the time was called generic form, such as linearity—as opposed to a specific line—and the idea of a process of form suggested by a relationship of form in space, such as rotation and shear, which again had nothing to do with the actual physical character of the form but with something implied in the relationship between forms. Previously, formal diagrams rarely discussed linearity or relationships in space and time. When they dealt with form as well as function, such diagrams became reductive geometric abstractions, ignoring such things as the critical thicknesses of walls and their possible effects as notations in space.

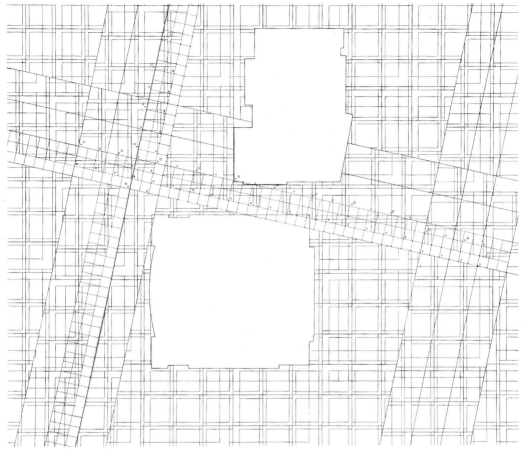

The diagrams in the Ph.D. thesis attempted to explain what I was only able to grasp intuitively. It was in these diagrams, particularly in those on the Italian architect Giuseppe Terragni, that the thesis came closest to revealing these intuitions. And even these diagrams have been revised and redrawn so many times over the last thirty years, that rendering any assessment of their original state, is now somewhat tentative. Nevertheless, given my lack of prior training in such matters, the diagrams in the thesis remain an important

initial document of my thinking about a relationship of built work to an architectural interiority.

My first two house projects were a further analysis of the relationship of architecture's interiority in relation to built form through the agency of the diagram. The idea was that the diagram could portray a logic analogous to an interiority of architecture. The change in the idea of the diagram in the five years between my Ph.D. thesis and the first houses is significant. The model for the new diagrams was clearly lin-

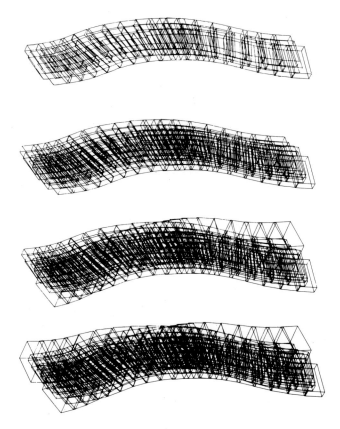

guistic as opposed to architectural-historical. These diagrams suggested not so much a stylistic expression in the reduction of the articulation of materiality in the built objects, as they did an idea to overcome presence. Thus the diagram could be marked and read in the built artifact.

In 1966 work began on my first house; actually, it was not a house but a toy museum as an extension to a house in Princeton, New Jersey. It was called House I (1968–69), a conceit used to distance the author, the subject, the client,

and the function from the architectural intention. Since there was no existing type for such a museum, the initial drawings for the house were a search for a diagram. These initial diagrams were used to draw into the project to find other diagrams. Once these were found, it was possible to work back to explain the diagram in terms of some basic geometry supposedly latent in any idea of an architectural interiority. What was meant at the time by "finding the diagram" was finding a method for getting from A to B in

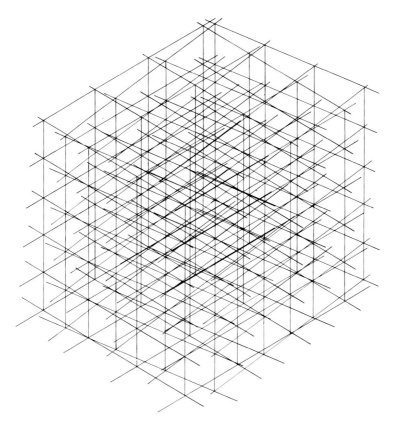

a rational way without resort to traditional design methods. The diagram was an attempt to relate an idea of an architectural interiority as it could be marked in the actual project. All specific forms were seen to be derived from an architectural interiority of cubes, rectangles, double cubes, etc., and their relationship to the specific project could be marked. Through the diagram, it was believed that a rational way could be found to get from A to B without the traditional aesthetic or functional decision-mak-

ing of the architect. It was assumed that diagrams A1, A2, A3, A4, A5 would somehow lead through a rational process to B. The diagram was a way of both searching for a process and explaining what was found.

This raises the question whether the diagrams of House I were *a posteriori*, that is, an attempt to explain or justify what had been done, or whether the project was one that resulted from the diagram. The search for the diagram in House I was similar to the search for the dia-

Interiority: Grids

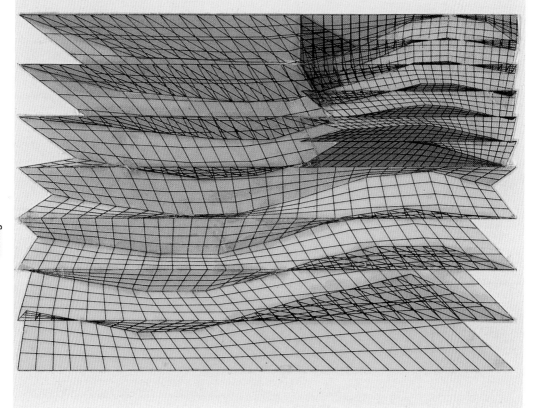

grams in the work on Terragni. With Terragni, the diagrams were an attempt to explain what was intuitively felt, which was not explainable in terms such as metaphysical, fascist, modernist, etc., usually used to refer to Terragni's work. In Terragni's Casa del Fascio, there were some articulations that could not be accounted for by structure, function, aesthetics, or symbolism. These articulations could be diagrammed, and the diagram was a way of uncovering the nature of their relationship to an architectural interiority.

The process in House I, while similar to the Terragni work, differed in the sense that there was no existing artifact. The diagram both found and explained simultaneously the relationship between an architectural interiority and a specific building.

For example, one of the House I diagrams marked on the floor a trace of a missing column. This signaled a reference in the actual space to some informing interior condition. This marking, which had nothing to do with

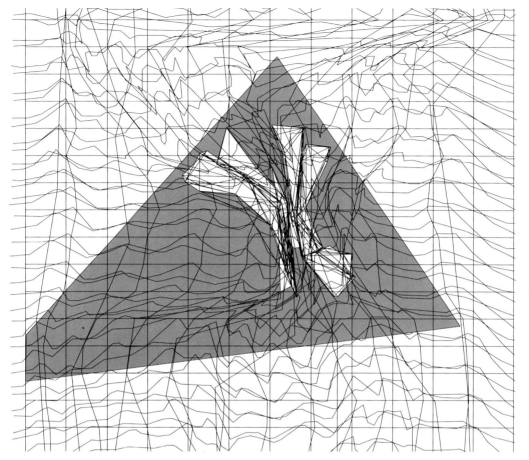

function or aesthetics, introduced the idea of absence of palpable presence in architecture in the form of a diagram. The specific articulation was the result of and marked the presence of a series of transformational diagrams that articulated a relationship to a series of anterior conditions always related to some primary forms. In essence, then, the earliest diagrams, which attempted to relate an architectural interiority to a built object, were also drawn from that interiority.

In addition to introducing the diagram, House I began to question the use of material structure as a primary expression. In any built work, while there were columns and beams—presences in the space—they were not holding anything up. These "structural" elements asked whether it was necessary to have a functioning structure in order to be necessarily iconic (i.e., to symbolize function). Was the actual material column to be considered merely a functional element or was it also a sign? Was the unstruc-

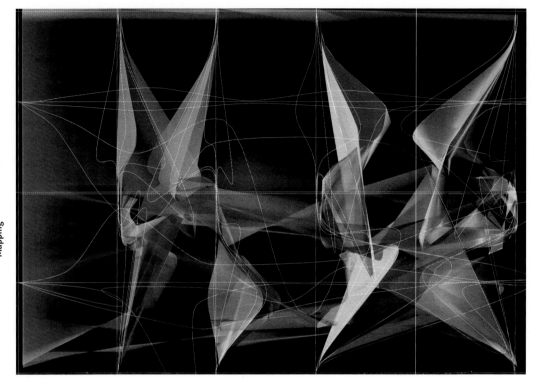

tural or "cardboard" column, since it was not a functioning structure, also a sign? Here, then, was the suggestion of the questioning of the physical with a sign structure signaled by the non-structural, both adding and subtracting structure, without any necessary function. The reduction of functioning materiality allowed for the possibility of other signs—perhaps the sign of the diagram—which could displace signs of function, aesthetics, and meaning in the built work. This displacement, proposed by the dia-

grammatic marks, questioned the nature of an interiority of architecture, which previously was assumed to have contained an essential functioning. It must be understood in the context of these early diagrams that the idea of a *deep structure* in the interiority of architecture was never meant to be synonymous with the idea of a formal essence, even though the actual diagrams contained unmistakable references to some valued formal origins, such as Platonic solids. Rather, the idea of deep structure as a prior

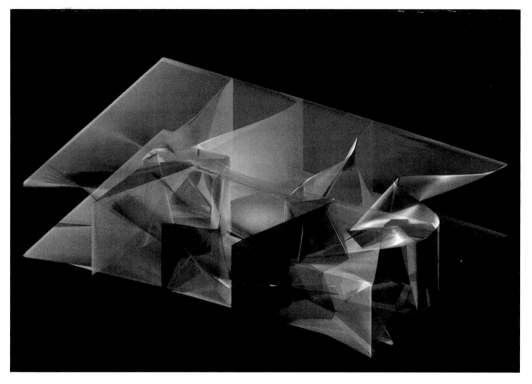

condition was intended to manifest an idea of architecture as an interiority of difference itself. It was a difference between form as embodying function and meaning to form as obedient only to its own formal condition. These early diagrams contained an assumption of a logic that no longer relied on formal essences, but rather on the possible aleatory conditions in the logic of the diagram itself. The diagram was an attempt to point to something previously unacknowledged in the modern project. And while

the formal vocabulary can be said to be the same, its polemical value was certainly modified by the diagram.

While the idea of a deep structure was defined by a set of logical relationships, the idea of marks of an absence in the building was intended first to move cognition from the built object to interiority and then to move the idea of interiority from one of formal essences to a diagram of potential otherness. It was argued that while all integers have a

Interiority: Cubes

Interiority: Cubes

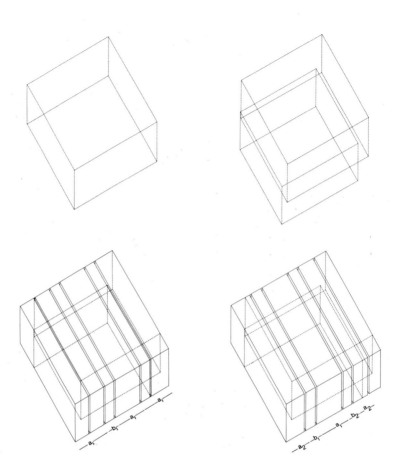

form, the aesthetic of the form, when seen in a diagram, is unimportant. Rather, the different positions in space and the inherent logic of their spatial relationships, of the so-called syntax of the diagram, would articulate some relationship to interiority when the integers of the diagram were placed in a real physical context. When these integers were absences as opposed to presences, these would signal a potential condition of original absence in interiority.

At the time, my use of the diagram was not so much an analogy as a proposal that these diagrams potentially existed in architecture. Their existence was repressed by the "natural" material, functional, and aesthetic conditions of architecture. In this sense, architecture's interiority was thought to be between diagram and type, but an idea of diagram as a difference, a difference other than architecture as function, style, or images. In House I and the series of early houses that followed, the diagram was thought to be comprising a set of existing

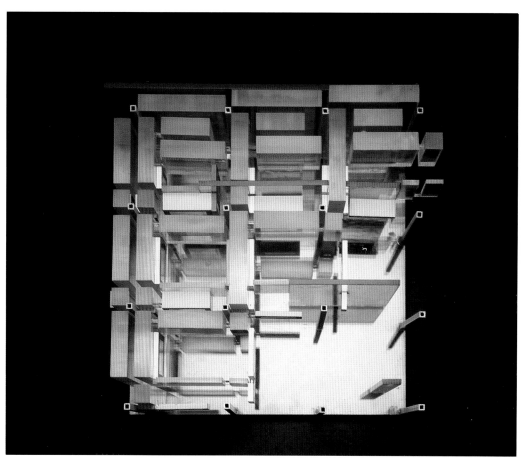

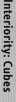

syntactic structures that informed any architecture. These regularities differed from the traditional idea of a formal essence in that they had no specific form attached to them, nor did they suggest any specific form, but rather could be considered as unformed possibilities for organization. These unformed possibilities of the diagram were not equivalent to the real space of architecture but were more like a Kantian schema.

In House II (1969–70), the diagrams initiated a discussion of self-referentiality and how such an idea might be manifested in architecture. In House II, self-referentiality was marked by an excess, as in the doubling of the structural system with both a column grid and a shear wall system, either of which would have been enough for structural support. It was argued that such an excess allowed one or the other of the structural systems to be seen as a sign, no longer referring to its structural value or to any external referent, but rather to an interiority. Since either column or wall

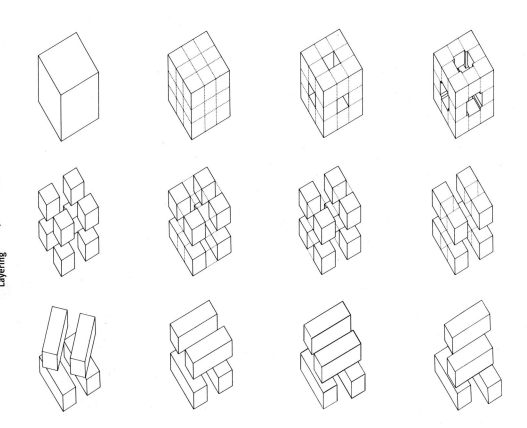

could be seen as a sign, there was no stable or unitary referent.

A self-referential sign was defined in the House II diagrams as the difference between an iconic sign and an indexical sign. Traditionally, the diagram had been used as an iconic sign—one which referred outward to some metaphoric existence. Now, the diagram was seen instead as a series of indexical signs: a system of differences that had little metaphoric or iconic content, but rather could be seen as a notational system understood as different from other formal systems. These indexical signs were thought to exist in some sort of suspension from their iconic condition yet as a potential condition of interiority. It was not that these indexical signs did not also have an iconic value, but this value could coexist with their indexical quality.

Any diagram in architecture will always be legitimated by function and meaning, which initially obscures any other intention. Obviously, all architecture can be seen as having something to

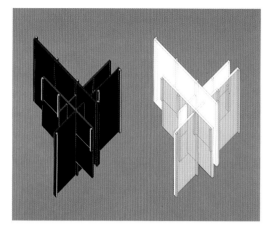
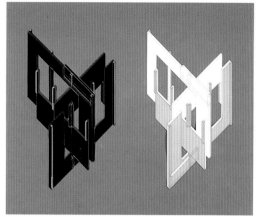

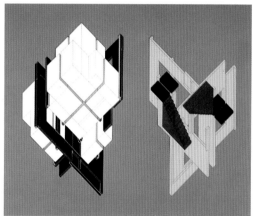

do with holding things up, with some intention to shelter, to enclose, and to divide, in short, fundamentally obeying the laws of gravity and statics. Thus columns and walls are rarely read initially as signs but more likely as integers of construction. It is not clear in this context whether lay people read them at all, either as construction or as signs of construction. This idea is supported by Walter Benjamin's thesis that architecture is viewed by an essentially distracted observer. The idea of the diagram as developed here proposed that architecture could exist as both integers of construction and also, on some level, as an index, that is, as the possibility to act as an *other* condition of sign that is not related to its function, its meaning, or its aesthetic. This *other* condition was characterized as one of an *excess* in relation to the necessary conditions of function, structure, and meaning. As an excess, it was then able to be seen as some form of potential *a priori* absence, because it was no longer tied to presence, i.e., construction, function, etc.

Interiority: Cubes

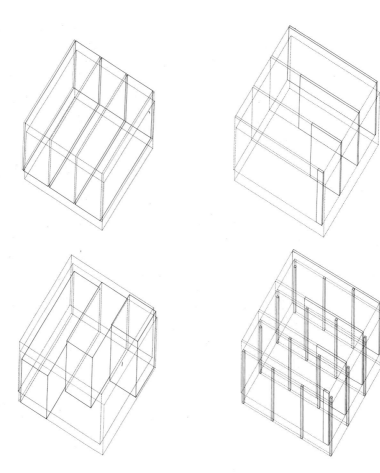

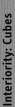

Thus in the House II diagrams, the particular integers—column, wall, etc.—were not seen as merely the sign of their class as integers of construction; they were also seen to represent something else. In order for this something else to take on a significance (a column is only a structural element until its dimensions are somehow marked or signed as something else), the column had to be designated in some way as other than structure. This designation of excess exists because either the grid of columns or the sequence of walls could be seen as an adequate structural system.

Taken together the two overlaid systems of House II blurred any relationship to an original value or single interpretation. The two systems were of equal value both formally and structurally, in that either the column or the wall could have been the operative structure. This could mean that either one system was not operative or each was operating at fifty percent, with half the loads being taken by the columns and half by the

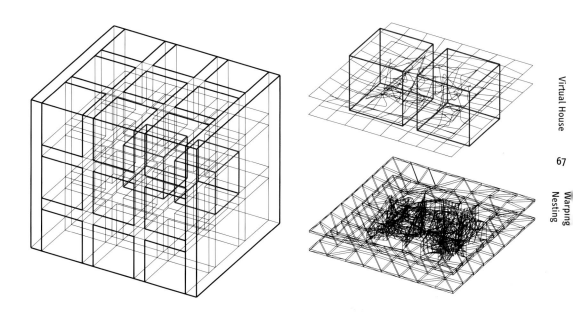

bearing walls. Either system could also be seen as an excess, causing one system to function as a sign as a result of a doubling of a structure. In House II, the built object becomes a diagram of the process. The object and the diagram are both one and the other; the real house operating simultaneously as a diagram.

Thus in the doubling of the structural system, the columns and the walls were no longer only formal or structural entities. Rather, as formal entities, they also marked an absence, the presence of interiority as mediated through the diagram. Indeed, the location of the columns or the walls was not seen to be the result of either formal or functional intentions, but rather the result of an indexical structure marking a redundancy of an excess which marked the presence (absence) of the diagram. The need to detach the icon from the instrument in order to read architecture not merely as a language but as a singular manifestation of an interiority of difference

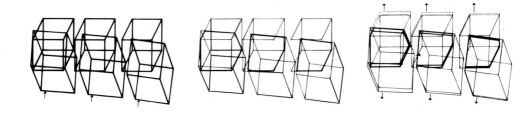

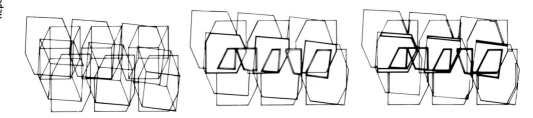

became an important part of the next series of diagrams.

House III (1969) departed from Houses I and II in that it attempted to blur the traditional hierarchy of perceptions of the real object, so that the diagrams could be more easily read in the actual building. In House II, a relationship was established between the physical object and an architectural interiority through the diagram. That relationship was then blurred by the creation of a possible dual origin. In House III, the diagrams attempted to blur the distinction between traditional primary, secondary, and tertiary visual readings. Where House II began with the structural system because it was the primary system of spatial organization, House III attempted to displace the idea of a primary structure. Here the columns, the room divisions—the walls—and the openings in the rooms were given equal valence. Since our way of reading architecture is to see things hierarchically—to read things as

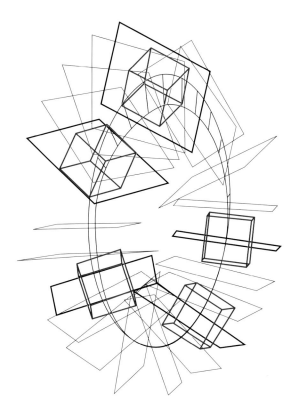

primary, secondary, and tertiary—the result of going against such hierarchical values was bound to be visually problematic. House III was no exception. This idea of confounding hierarchical perception opened up new ground in that in its blurring of what is seen, it also suggested that such a blurring of hierarchy was a condition of architecture's interiority. But in each of the first three houses, the diagrams assumed that a formal and geometric content were at the core of any architectural interiority.

House IV (1971) was the first purely diagrammatic project. Its series of diagrams were concerned not only with the hierarchy of the integers of construction but also with their materiality. The House IV diagrams concerned the *being* of the diagram, such as the idea of *wallness*, as opposed to a mere plane. This was the first indication of the potential for affect to influence the diagram. The sign of wallness demanded overcoming not only the materiality of the object but also its function and meaning.

Interiority: El-Forms

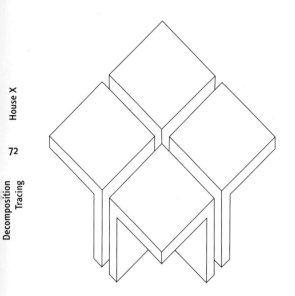

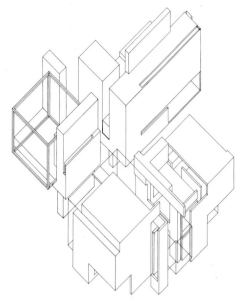

The necessity of overcoming the materiality of architecture was also seen as part of architecture's singular interiority. Therefore, the term *wallness*, as opposed to *planeness*, was introduced into the diagrammatic process to denote the need to overcome the problem of materiality in architecture, as opposed to the problem of materiality in painting or sculpture. Planeness, it was argued, described the being of sculpture or painting but did not describe the being of architecture. Wallness, on the other hand, articu-

lated the difference between architecture and sculpture in that it is a paradoxical condition of the vertical plane in which the sign must overcome function and meaning in order to become architecture. However, without function and meaning there would be no conditions that would require such an intentional act of overcoming. Here, in the idea of overcoming, architecture is no longer a relationship of an *a priori* essence to an object but a condition in real time and space. In this context, the diagram becomes

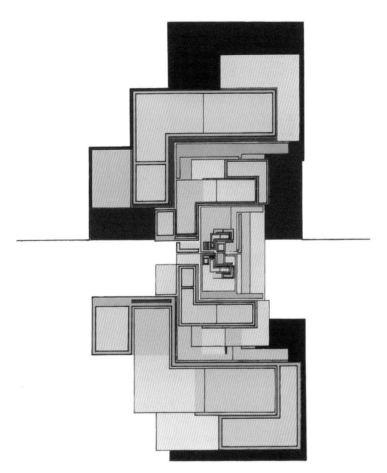

both substance and act—"the sign as a record of an intervention, an act which goes beyond the presence of elements which are merely necessary conditions." The notion of such an act in the early houses was seen as a diagram of excess.

The diagrams of House IV proposed a sign system that refers to this most primitive condition of architecture, distinguishing it from the simple equation of geometry plus function and meaning. These two conditions of diagram, function and meaning, need to be distinguished from a third condition of the architectural object, which at the time was called *presentness*. Presentness in this context is described as nothing more than an act, an event of signing that is manifest in real space/time with no reference to the future or the past. The conditions for presentness as a condition of architectural time, or architecture as a condition of act, are present in the diagram seen as an indexical sign. The indexical sign, which always implies a condition of absence, suggests an idea of time in the diagram.

It is the nature of an indexical sign that leads to an idea of absence. When the diagram becomes indexical, that is, a self-referential sign, the idea of the diagram shifts again from a linguistic analogy to the possibility of the affective. Here, then, is another transition, the first from architecture as form to architecture as language, and now to architecture as a condition of affect. Thus, as an event of signing, the diagrams of House IV also implied a condition of excess beyond the necessity of function. This idea of excess was different

from those of House II primarily because the diagrams of House IV were, for the first time, not merely an *a posteriori* explanatory device but also a generative device. The diagrams began from a series of rule systems that once set in motion would begin to change the very nature of the rule system itself. The generative rule system would bring about a series of moves, like in a game of chess, in which each move is a response to the last. With each move the system produces different alternatives and then readjusts

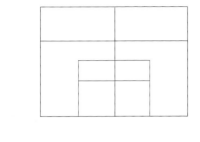

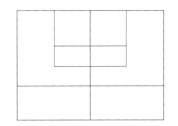

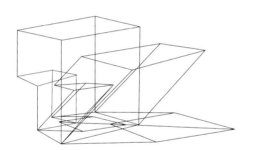

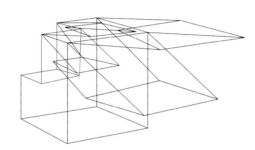

itself. The end product could not have been pre-dicted in advance. Here, the subject's desire for a pre-figured result is blunted.

What seemed to be a logical set of moves, however, was shown to be flawed in a film of the diagrams for Aldo Rossi's 1973 Triennale in Milan. Over one thousand frames were drawn and assembled into what was called a "flicker film." Each blank, black frame was followed by a white frame of an image, causing the images to pulsate. The drawings produced what seemed to

be a linear narrative of a process. When the dia-grams were arranged to be seen in a single view, they could be understood as a narrative. This was because the eye, when looking at two drawings, one beside the other, attempts to make a connection of its own to fill in the gap between the drawings even if there is no con-nection. For example, in morphing techniques, object A can be turned into a different object B through the creation of intermediate stages. In the film there were such intermediary stages:

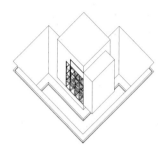

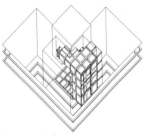

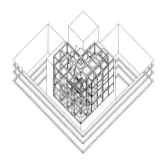

because of the flicker, the eye did not have time to make the connections, and because there were no connections between what the eye saw and what was recorded in the mind, what was seen seemed unintentionally chaotic.

Vision always attempts to make order out of chaos; in the process of diagramming, it is necessary to reduce the impact of this natural tendency to order what is seen. The diagrams of House IV have an order that is not only visible and able to be put together logically by the seeing eye. They are also a trace of a nonlinear, nonhierarchical process that cannot be taken back to zero. This became clear in the attempt to present them in the linear format of the flicker film.

House VI (1972–75) used the diagram to develop further an idea of a filmic process. Film is itself a summation of frames. Thus to see the diagrams as a summation of the house, rather than seeing them essentially as individual stills leading to a conclusion, required a different idea

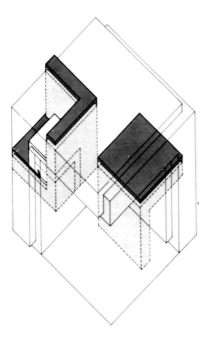

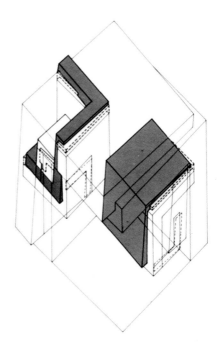

of process. In all of the previous work, including House IV, the house was a linear transformation from A to B. House VI attempted to reveal these stages as compressed into a single time frame. In the built object, color was introduced into the diagrams because such a co-temporality could not be explained in black and white.

In the earlier houses, the diagrams were understood as colorless and essentially unconcerned with materiality. That immateriality was expressed as part of the coding of the house, as a representation of the diagrammatic process. Since House VI was no longer a representation of the diagrammatic process but in fact was the process itself, another coding was required, that is, coloring not only the diagrams but also the house. In addition, the coding was important to indicate levels of solid and void. As in House IV, the diagrams indicated wall surfaces by the notations solid, double solid, neutral solid, single void, and double void.

While House IV was the first attempt to code the materiality of the house in the diagram, it was necessary for House VI to also code the shift from Euclidean geometry to topological geometry. This shift had to be understood in the actual experience of the house, and not only in the diagrams. The house was keyed along a topological axis that ran from one corner in the top rear to one corner in the bottom front, through a diagonal center. In order to articulate this axis, two staircases were painted red and green; mixing red and green produces the gray of the neutral axis of the house. Since white had been the base color for the first four houses, gray now became the neutral color marking the central topological axis. In this context, white became one pole, a point at the center, there was a gray line as the neutral axis, and black was the other pole, an imagined exterior enclosure. Red and green, then, were the signs of an unseen, yet conceptual neutral topological axis.

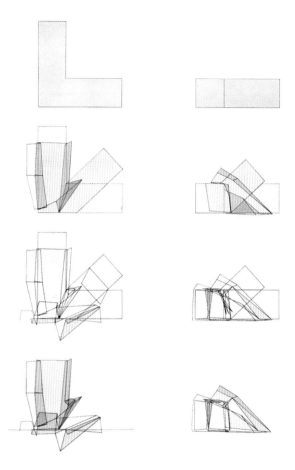

Interiority: El-Forms

If the red staircase had been made parallel to and directly above the green staircase, it would have been symmetrical in Euclidean space. When the red staircase was turned ninety degrees, it became asymmetrical in Euclidean space but topologically symmetrical along a line from the bottom corner of the house to its top corner. The red and green stairs keyed the idea that there was a gray topological axis. Once that was read, there was no longer a right side up or an upside down in the house; the house became

reversible in its orientation, bearing no conceptual relationship to the ground. This was another step in the process of moving away from ground as a defining condition of architecture. In House IV, while there was an actual Euclidean geometry of the space, the understanding of the space could only be topological. The house made no conceptual sense when experienced with Euclidean coordinates. The front and rear exterior vertical surfaces (there were no facades) were inversions of each other. Moving from the

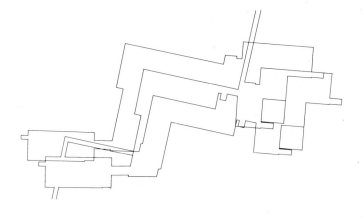

front to the back through the conceptual layers, one was moving from something which seemed right side up to upside down. The house not only was upside down topologically, but also inside out. In the middle of the gray line, which was the topological axis, was a white dot as the generating trace of the house. Surrounding the gray line was a black box. The conception thus was from a black box through a gray line to a white dot. All vertical and horizontal surfaces in the house were colored various shades of gray.

This same marking device was also operative in the material surfaces. As one moved out from the white point, the glass planes became more opaque, moving from transparent, to translucent, to gridded translucency, to opacity. Thus, all of the material vertical and horizontal surfaces and their cuts were coded in an index.

House VI became a kaleidoscope of diagrams rather than the result of a generative sequence. The diagrams were not the house itself. The house itself did not need to be the diagram, the

summation of the process, or the last diagram, yet at the same time the house was required to manifest all its diagrams. In this context, House VI was the end of a particular process. All of the previous houses had been generative transformations from some pure geometric origin. After House VI, another idea of a diagrammatic process was initiated. It was a process of suspension, a taking of something that existed and making it palpable through a process that at the time was called *decomposition*.

With the idea of decomposition, the dominating processes of transformation were put into question. This began through my work on Terragni's Giuliani-Frigerio apartment block in Como, Italy. No longer was it felt necessary to understand architecture's interiority as a cube, a double cube, or a half-cube and to transform them. Rather it was thought possible to begin from a state of complexity. The residue of this complexity was conceptualized like a chemical suspension taken to

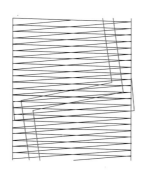
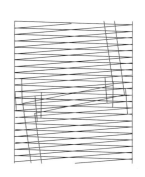

Interiority: El-Forms

some form of recognition or palpability. The palpability could not be taken either to a degree zero, to an origin, or to its former state of complexity. There was enough in its presence to suggest movement in the direction of a zero state without necessarily ever being able to reach it conceptually. When such an explanation was attempted, something else would become unexplainable. If the procedure was reversed and the unexplainable became explainable, then something else would fail to make any sense. There was constant oscillation of a moving in and out of focus. No longer was the diagram trying to explain a unitary origin in which the only explanation possible was a diagram originating from a pure geometry. Rather, the diagram contained a manifold condition of *unformed matter* from which one could suspend material in a frozen moment in time and space. Interiority, then, was no longer conceptualized as formed, but in fact was seen as a condition closely akin to complex matter.

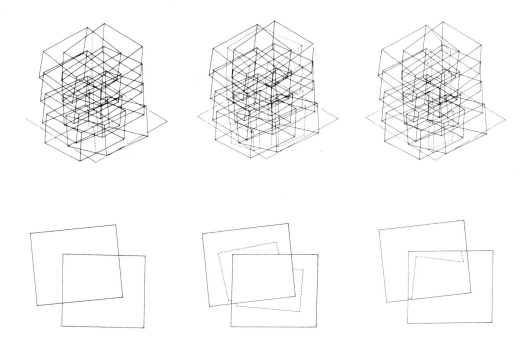

This opened up a way of thinking through a diagrammatic process that became House X.

The diagrams of House X (1975–78) attempted to produce a condition in space that could no longer be read hierarchically from some simple geometric origin even though it appeared to read from such an origin. Each time a reading from a unitary beginning was attempted, the explanation would fail. The diagrams led back not to an origin but to a diffuse condition in space and time which was no longer holistic, hierarchical, or stable, but constantly fluctuating.

These diagrams were initially based on an idea of topological space developed in House VI. In House X, the idea was that there were two incomplete origins—an el cube and an el point, each missing a quadrant. The el form moved toward both a black cube and a white point. Both of these operations were endpoints of equal validity. House X, like House VI, thus manifested a coding that went from black through gray to white.

Interiority: El-Forms

Interiority: Bars

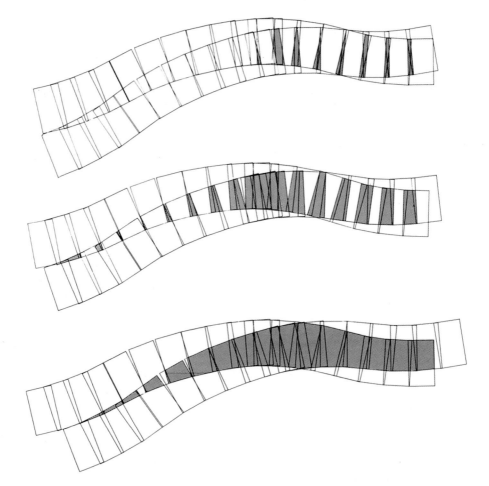

As a series of diagrams they did not move progressively. Each time they moved toward a unitary condition in space or time, they were destabilized. This was similar to the diagrams of Terragni's Giuliani-Frigerio, which began from topological corners. The Giuliani-Frigerio was explained not from the facades, as with the Casa del Fascio, but from the corners.

Traditionally in architecture there were two preferred points of reading for the subject: either frontal (as in the Renaissance) or from the corner (as in neoclassicism). In a frontal building, a reading from the corner adds nothing to the conceptual understanding of the building. The dominant reading is from the center of the front facade. In neoclassicism, the side facades and the front facades were conceived as folding out from the corner to create a unitary whole. In the Casa del Fascio, there are frontal readings as well as a series of readings from the corner. This produces a condition where the subject is required to move around the building

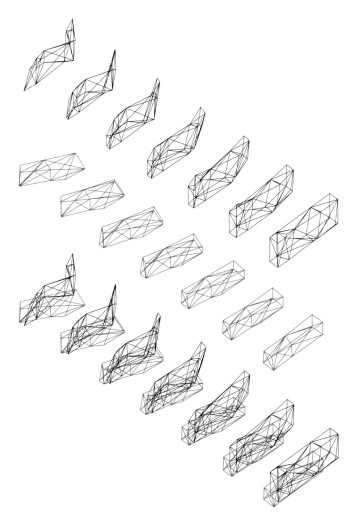

in a sequence from front to corner, from side to corner, and from back to corner.

The diagrammatic work on House X evolved from a similar idea of reading between a single viewpoint and multiple viewpoints. In addition, the diagrams also worked between topological geometry and Euclidean geometry, between a single subject and a multiple subject. In House X there were multiple viewpoints from the corners and the centers and also from the inside. The house was divided into quadrants so that the viewing subject not only stood outside but inside at the point of topological symmetry.

The diagrams of House X again suggested the idea that the interiority of architecture might not be something stable and already known. Previously, the diagrams of the early houses related the physical object to a stable and known universe similar to the trajectory of interiority from the Renaissance through modernism. While the styles of architecture may have changed, the universe from which the

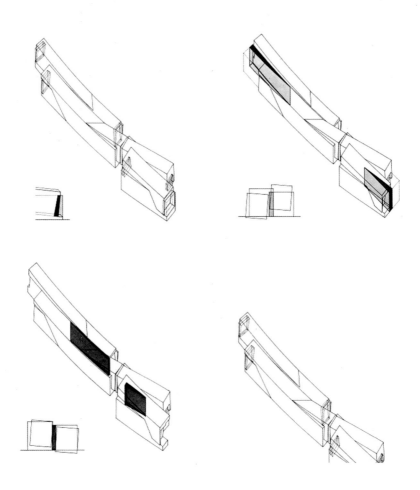

forms were drawn was seen to be stable. In House X, the diagrammatic index could no longer present a one-to-one representation of what constituted the nature of this unstable interiority. For example, when the geometry of the interiority was Euclidean, it could appear on a piece of paper as its own representation. When the geometry became topological, it could no longer be represented on a flat piece of paper in a one-to-one relationship. So the diagrams began to move from icons of this Euclidean interiority to indices of a topological geometry drawn as Euclidean because of the limitations of existing drawing methods.

The naming of House El Even Odd (1980) dealt with some of the conceptual issues of the project. The "El" comes from the el forms of House X; the "El Even" for the number eleven in the series, and also for the Kabbalistic number for the beginning, the end, and the beginning again; and "Odd" for a new sequence of odd and even as opposed to a linear numerical sequence.

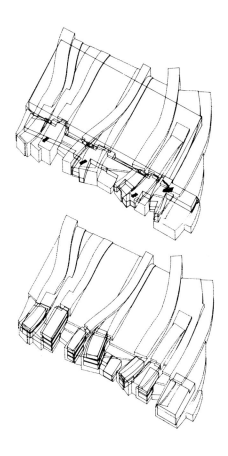

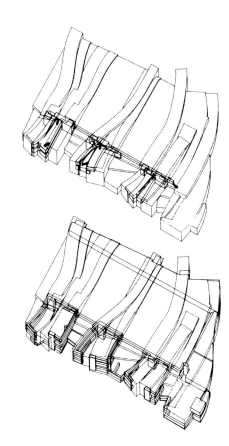

The project concerned the dominance of the human subject's perspectival view in relation to the object. The project began from the axonometric model that was built for House X. The model, when viewed in a monocular fashion from a certain viewpoint, could be seen as a "real" model. Its walls appeared to be vertical and horizontal, like a real model, giving the idea that reality and axonometric projections are somehow involved with one another. House El Even Odd took this idea as its diagram and developed it through three stages of axonometry. The first stage was an orthogonal projection using one of the pavilions from House X. The second stage was an axonometric projection of the same pavilion tipped at a forty-five-degree angle, and the third stage was an axonometric projection of the second-stage axonometric, which produced, oddly enough, a flat planlike plane.

The result was a three-dimensional volumetric overlay of the three stages. Upside down and reversed, it produced a condition in which all

Interiority: Bars

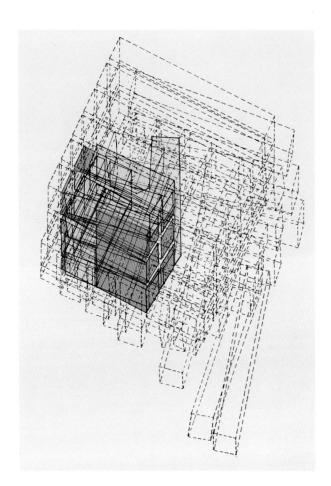

that was seen, upon coming upon the house, was a plan. Thus, the house was first read as a plan, even though this perception was in fact the third stage of transformation of an original volume. In this way, the overlay of the diagram confounded the perception of axonometry and stereotomy—that is, regular orthogonal projections of plans with perspectival readings of the same.

The diagrams of House El Even Odd were seen to present a continuing transformation of the idea of the architectural sign with respect to the idea of dwelling. In House El Even Odd the diagram became the sign of the sign of the program and the idea of dwelling as both intransigent and malleable. When the three-stage diagrammatic projection became self-reflexive, it existed not only as an object but also as its own representation. It was argued that the shift from an architecture that imitates nature to one that represents its own object was required in order to dislocate the traditional need to make dwelling, and thus to displace an interiority of

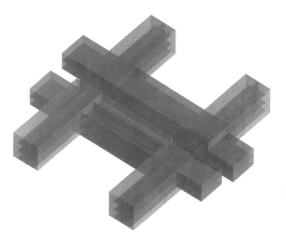

Interiority: Bars

architecture traditionally seen as a stable relationship between form and function. It is this stability that leads to the impossibility of making any
modification in the typology of dwelling. It was
thought that this relationship could be destabilized, then the making of architecture could be
something that is both dwelling as well as a sign
of something else—the presentation of a diagram as an aspect of architecture's interiority.

The house, i.e., dwelling, is in one sense the
locus of memory and therefore represents "the
constant sign of the nostalgia for dwelling."
While in House El Even Odd there were neutral signs that corresponded to a maximum
absence of imagery, it was thought that this
absence would signify the absence of the traditional form/dwelling relationship. The idea of
absence as the sign of an *other* presence of a
destabilized interiority, that is, as a presence in
architecture without its traditional legitimation
in the function of dwelling, presented a different
idea of absence than had been thought of previ-

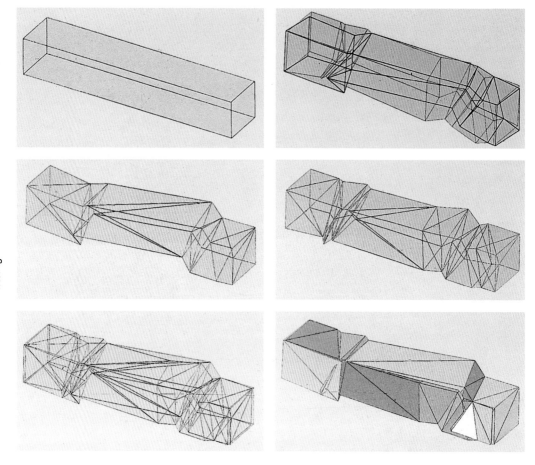

ously. This displacement, projected from the earliest house projects to House El Even Odd, was seen as one that moved the interiority of architecture from the idea of the house as the sign of dwelling to the house that is only a sign, a representation only of itself.

The Fin d'Ou T Hous (1983) represented another break from the earlier houses. This was seen in the particular relationship of the diagram to the project. The early houses were transformations and records of those transforma-

tions; they related the formal interiority of architecture to the formal condition of the house itself. These houses were mostly based in Euclidean geometry. The Fin d'Ou T Hous was the first house that was declared at the time to be a writing. The first writing was in its name, which provoked different readings. It could be read as "Find Out House," "Fine Doubt House," or even "Fin d'Août," the end of August, which was the time of its making. The house was about a notion of writing as an

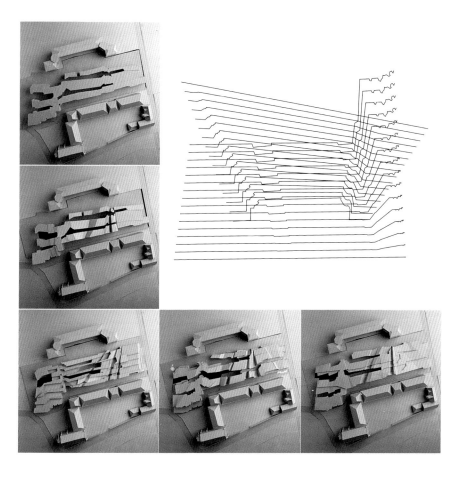

index. In order to mark this index, a series of transformational diagrams was produced using the el form as a topological counter. This house again marked an uncertain beginning: it started from both a point and a full cube. This thinking, which began in Houses VI and X, exhausted itself in this house.

The diagrams of the Fin d'Ou T Hous worked on many different levels. They evolved from the relationship of the diagram to the house, that is, the way the diagrams are marked

in House IV. Essentially the idea was to produce a set of diagrams so that any attempt to trace its transformations from some origin was problematized. The diagrams indicated a possibility to be read and traced, but as in a bad mystery novel all of the clues, when traced to their origin, proved to be false. Instead, these clues led only to another system of tracking that would take one in another direction. This was similar to the process of decomposition that had begun with House X.

House I 1967–68

96

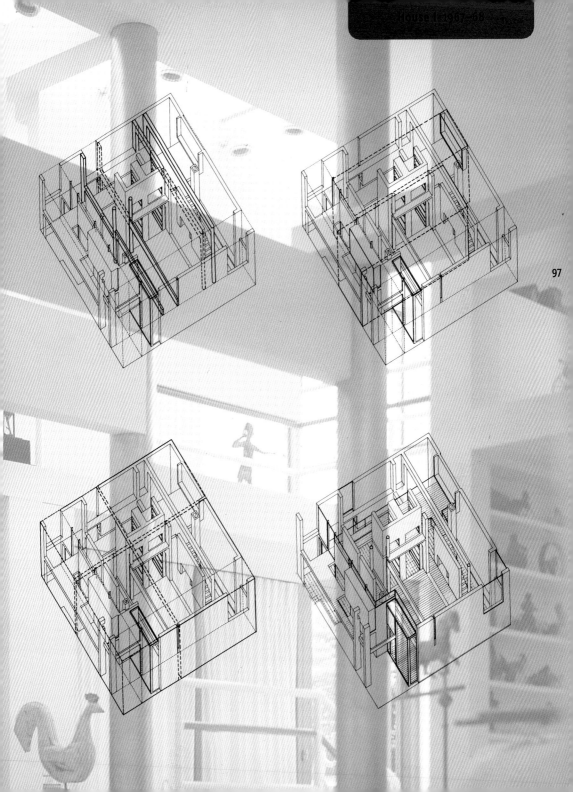

100

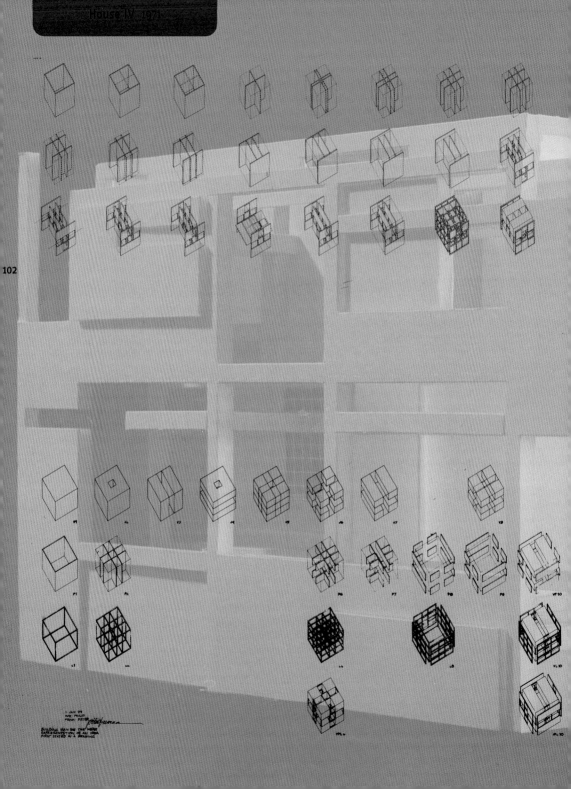

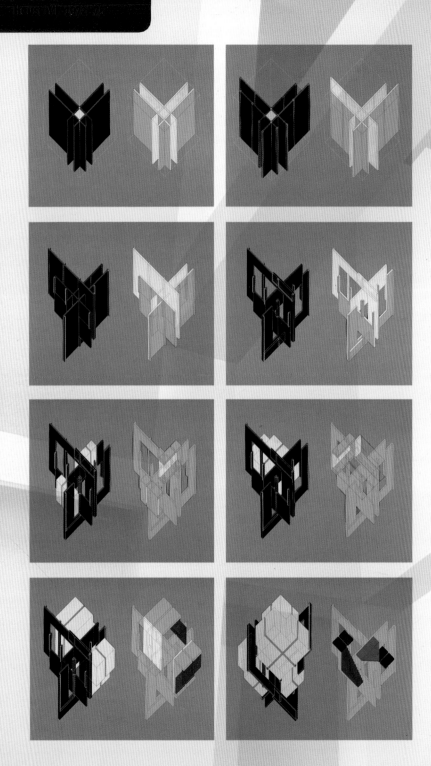

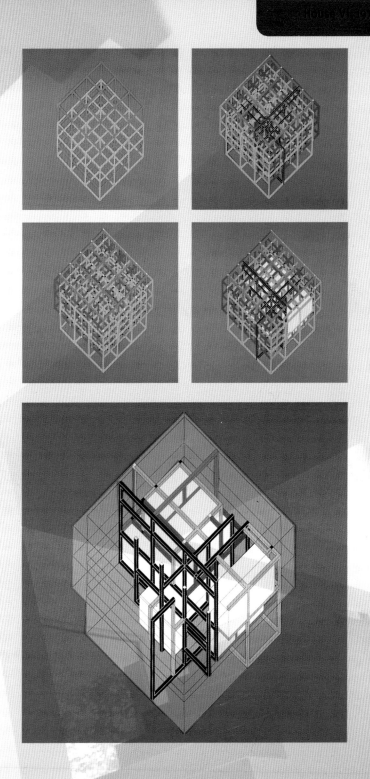

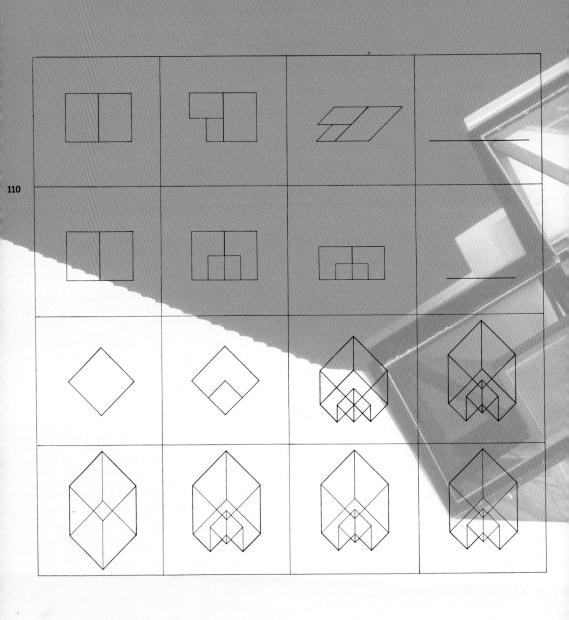

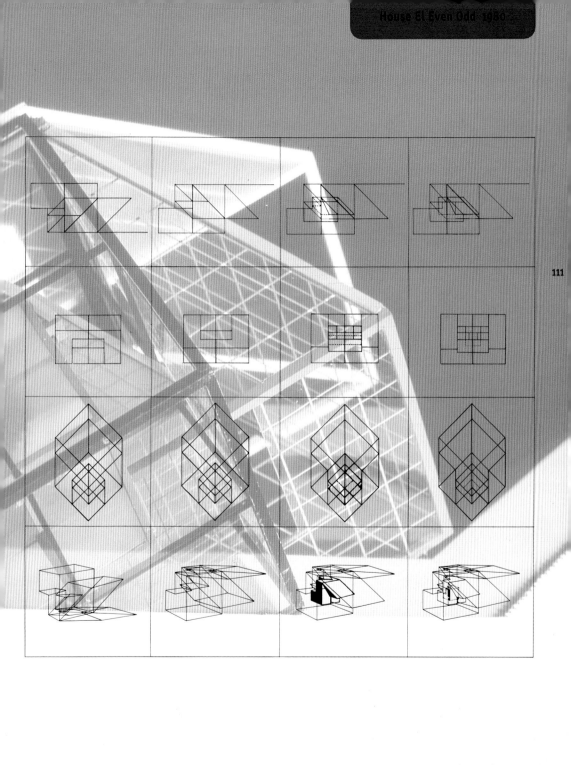

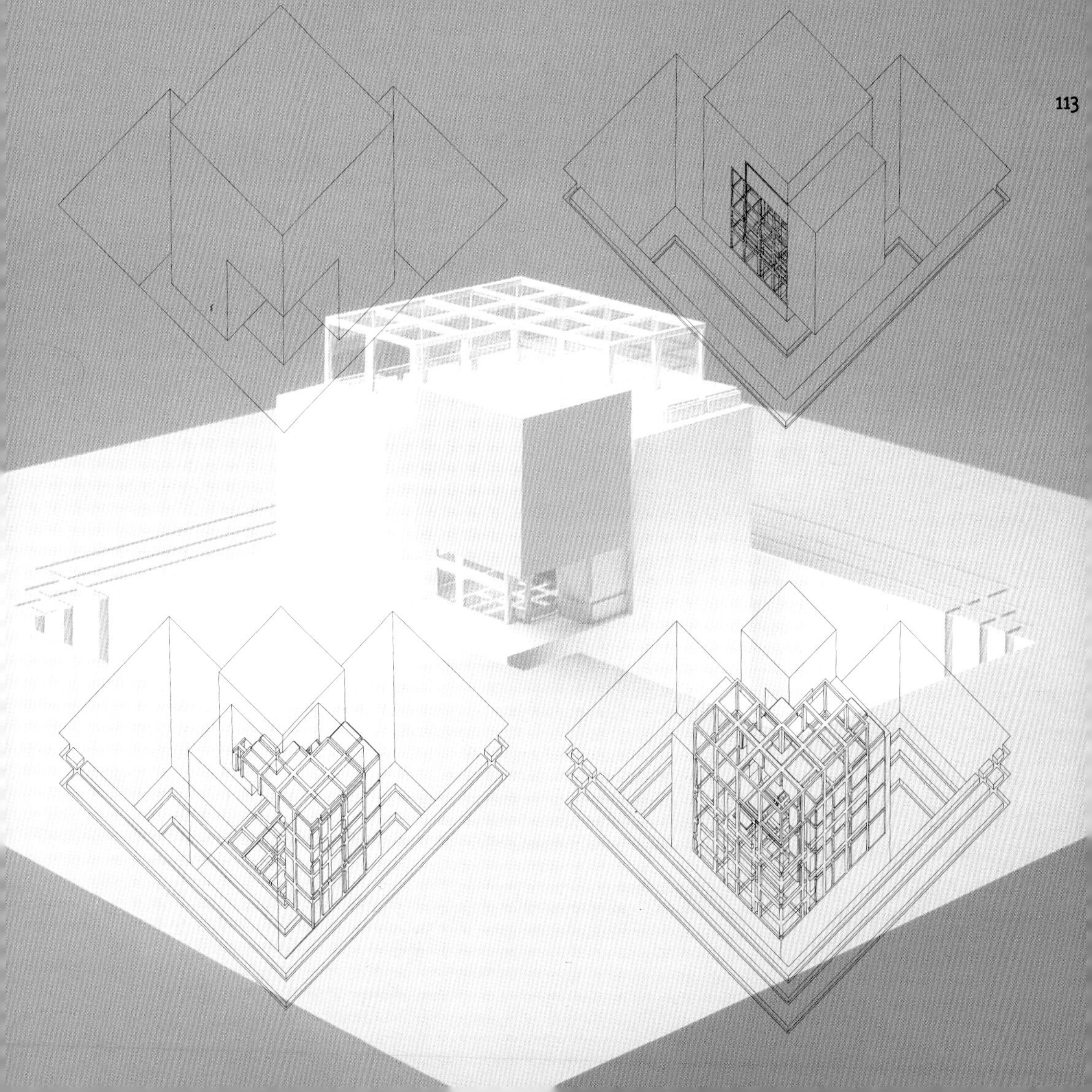

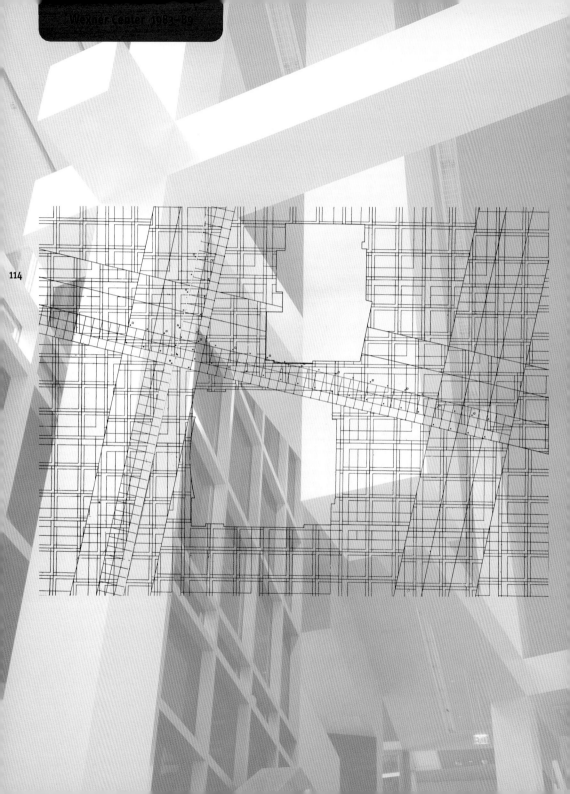

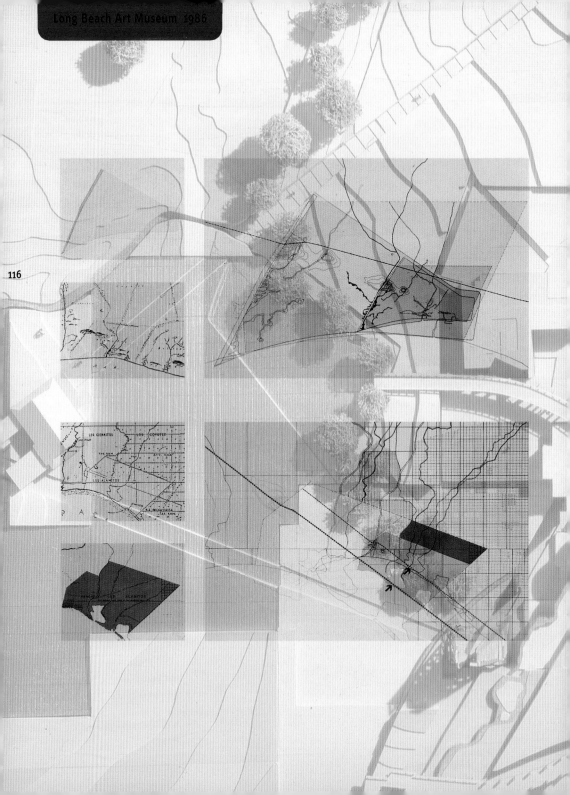

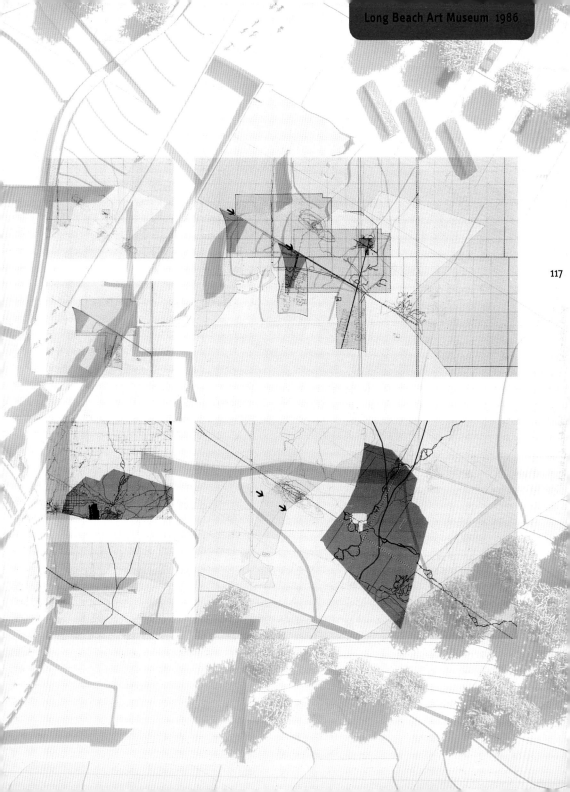

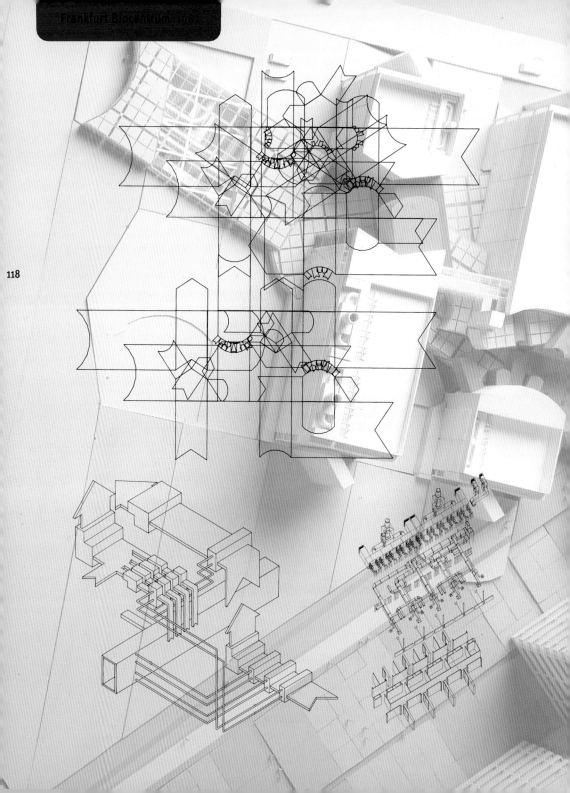

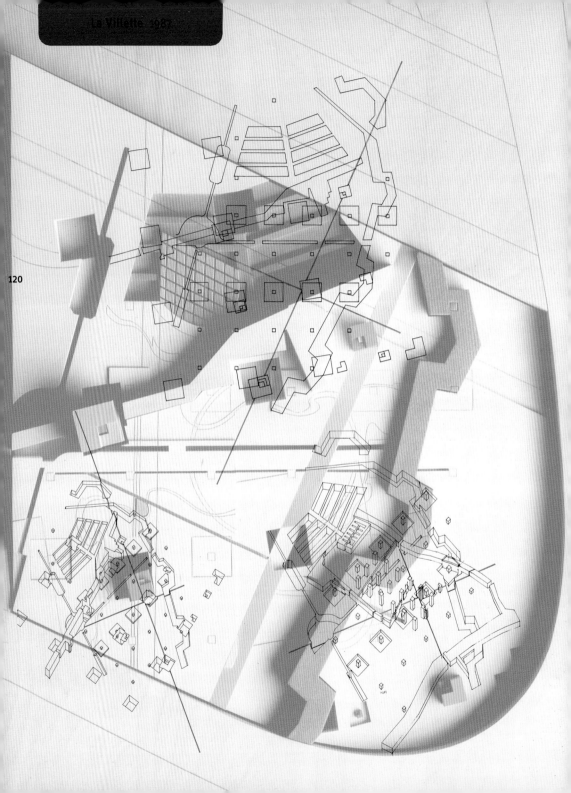

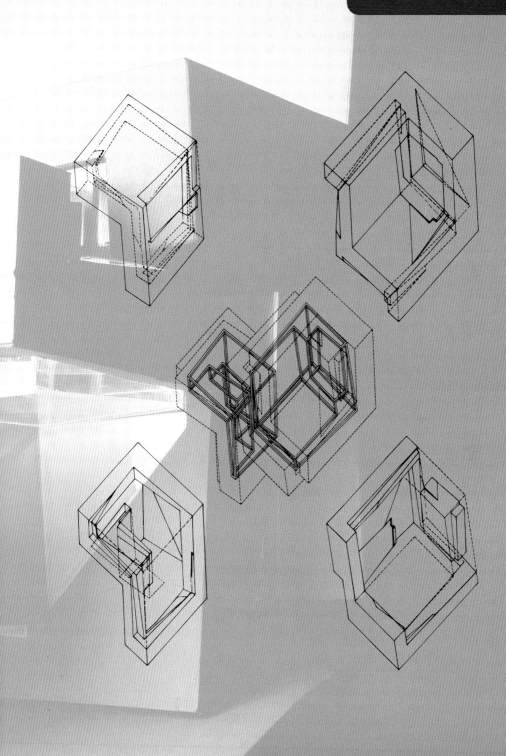

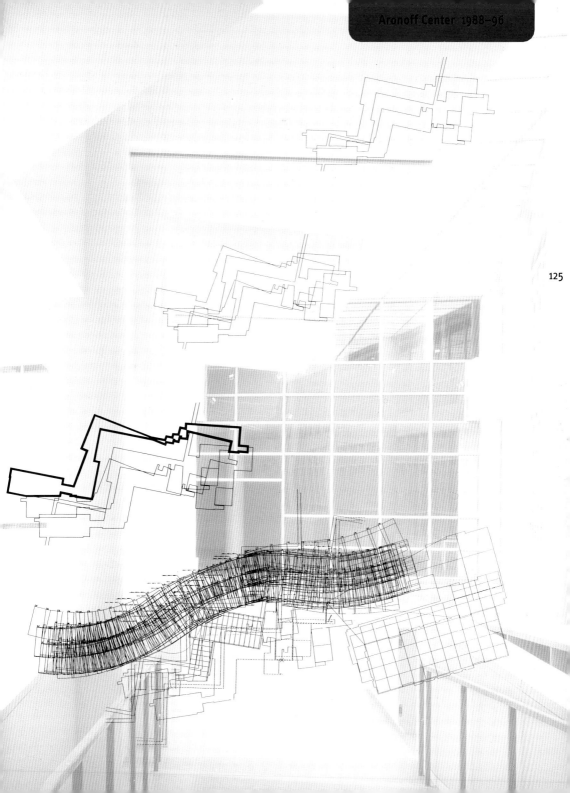

127

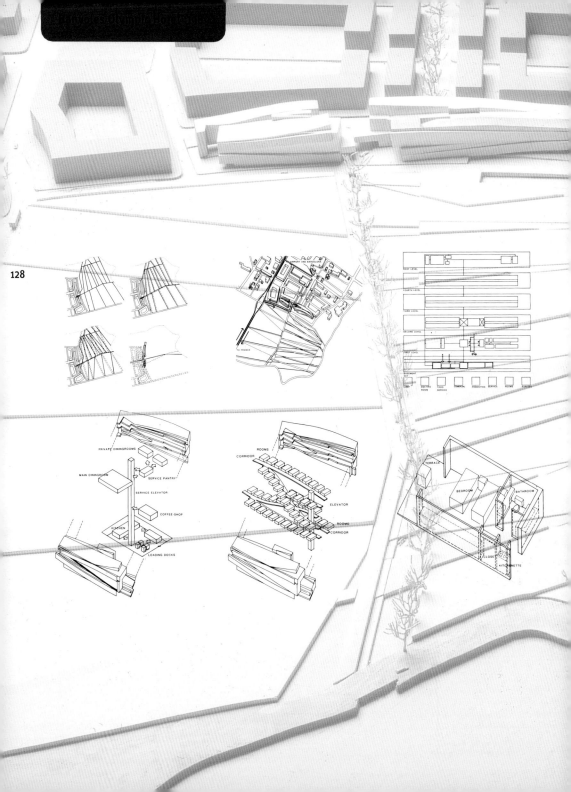

128

ROOF LEVEL

FOURTH LEVEL

THIRD LEVEL

SECOND LEVEL

FIRST LEVEL

BASEMENT

MEETING ROOM   FOOD SERVICE   COMMERCIAL   AMENITIES   SERVICES   ROOMS   PARKING

AIRPORT AND BARCELONA

TO FRANCE

PRIVATE DININGROOMS

MAIN DININGROOM

SERVICE PANTRY

SERVICE ELEVATOR

COFFEE-SHOP

KITCHEN

LOADING DOCKS

ROOMS

CORRIDOR

ELEVATOR

ROOMS

CORRIDOR

TERRACE

BEDROOM

BATHROOM

CLOSET

KITCHENETTE

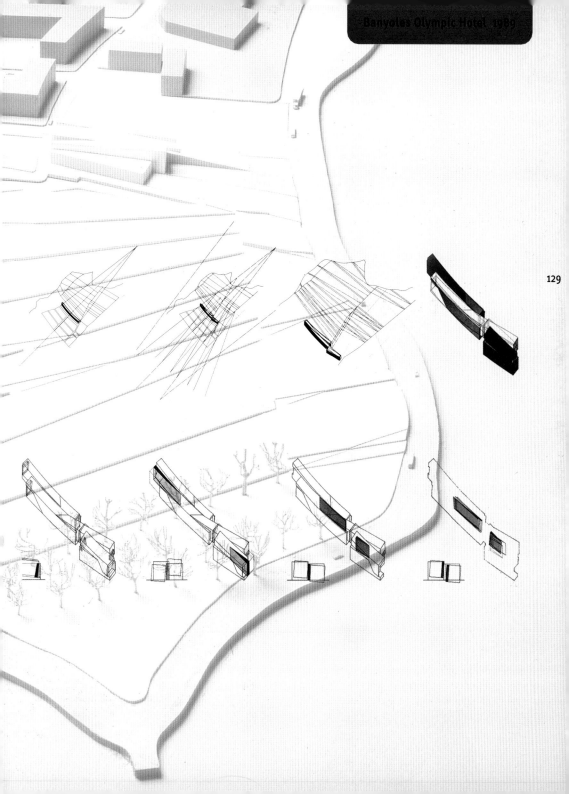

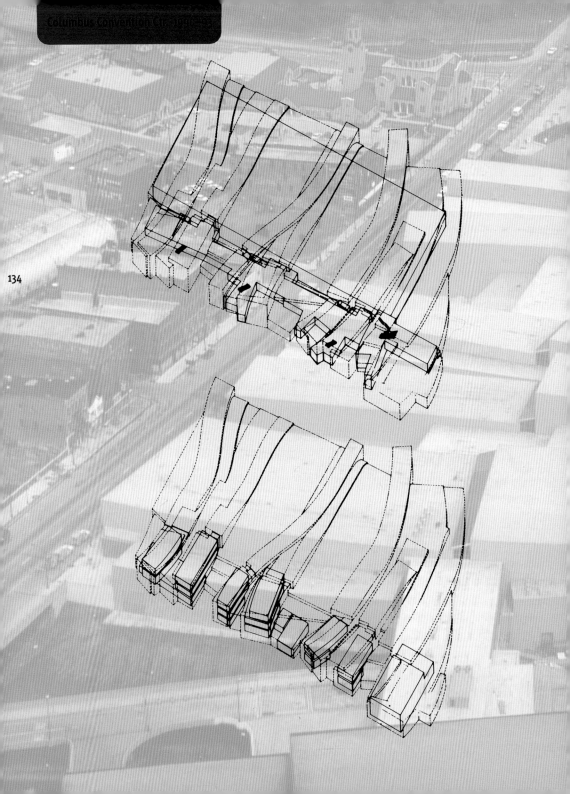

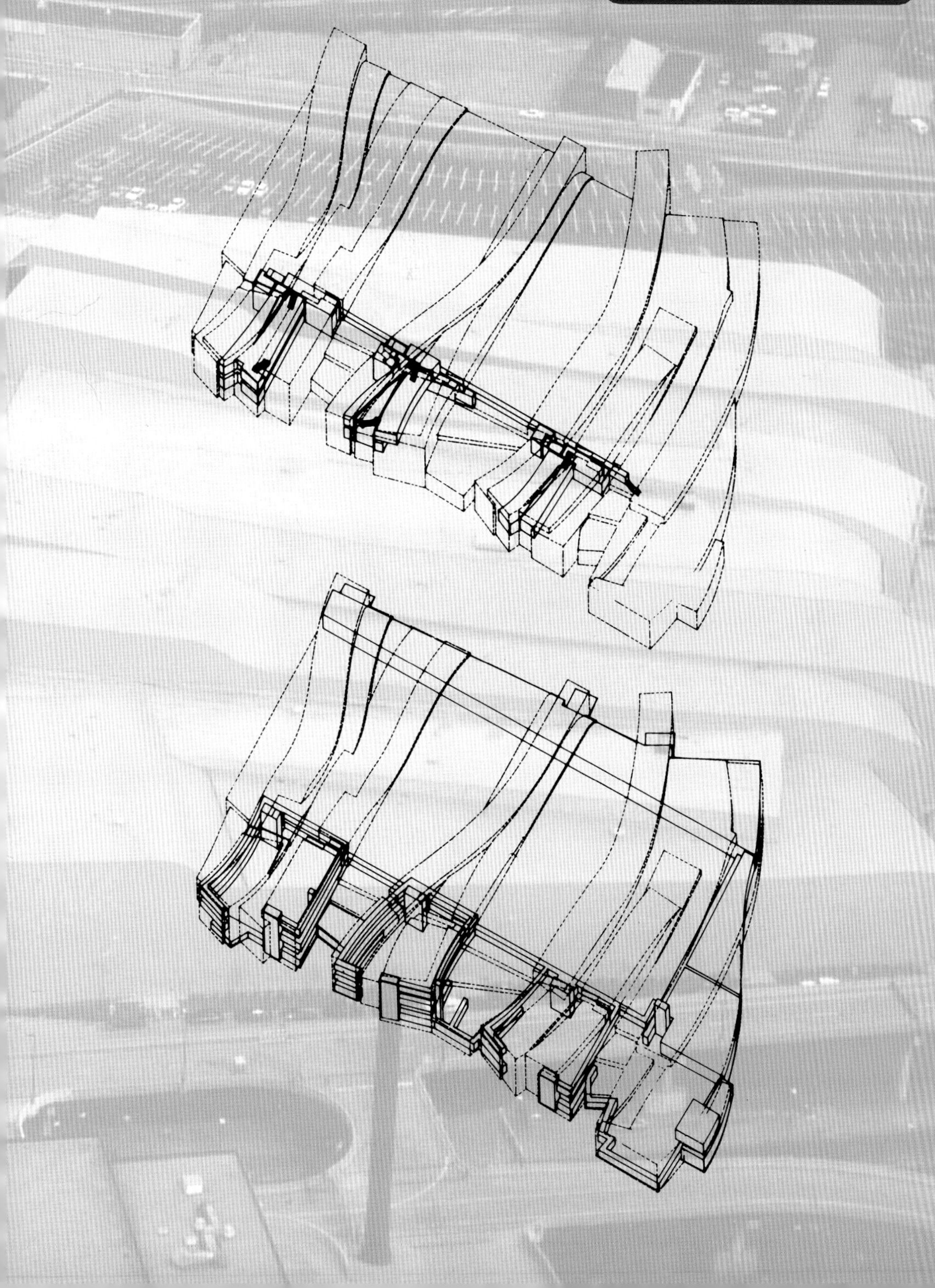

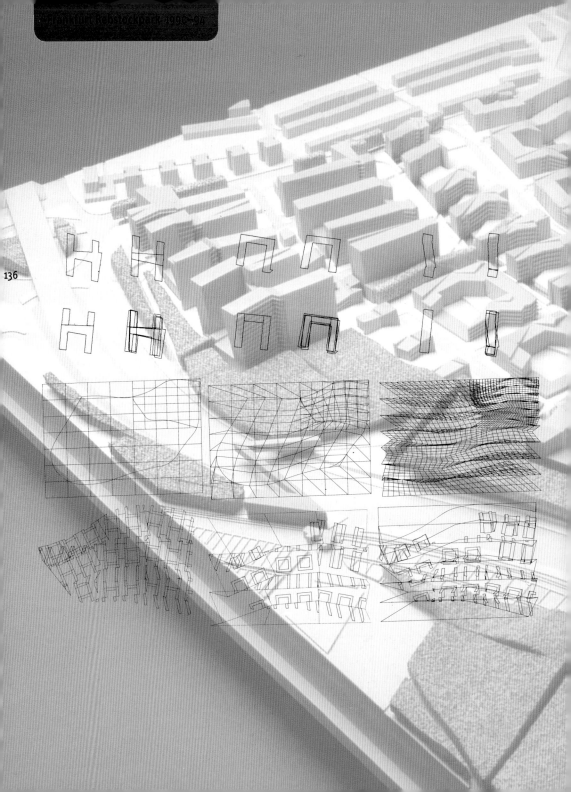

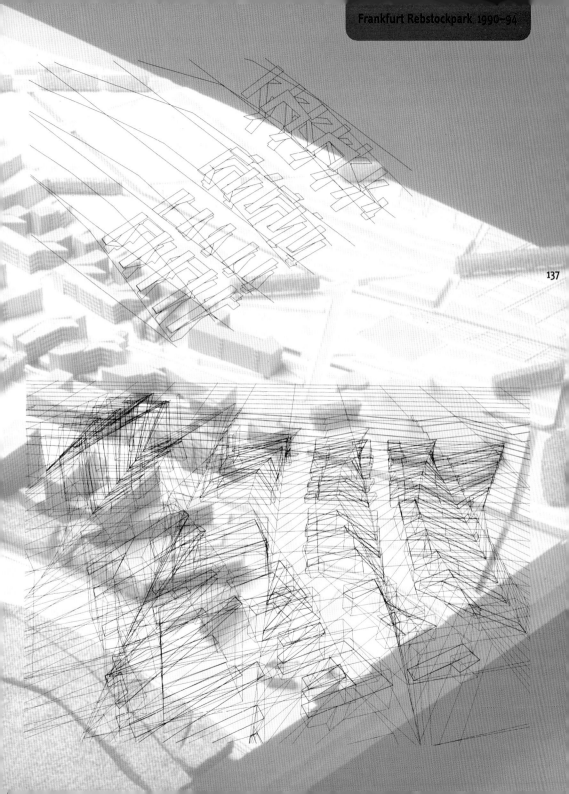

138

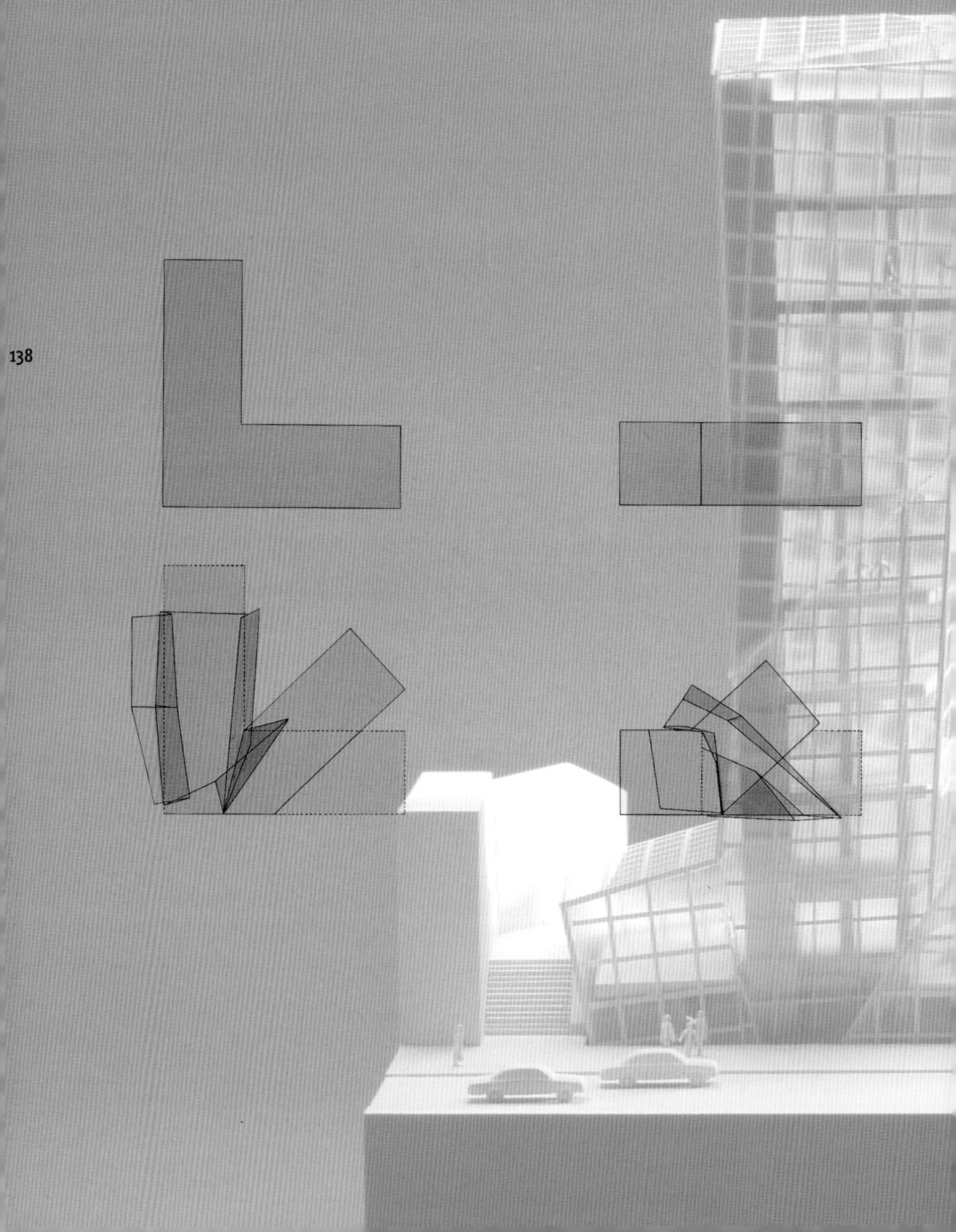

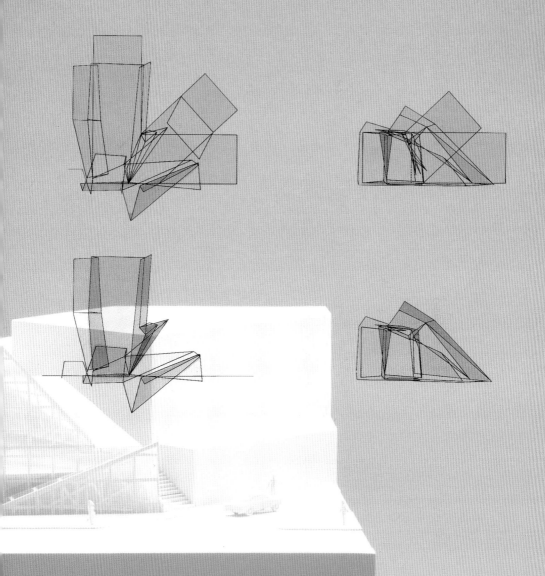

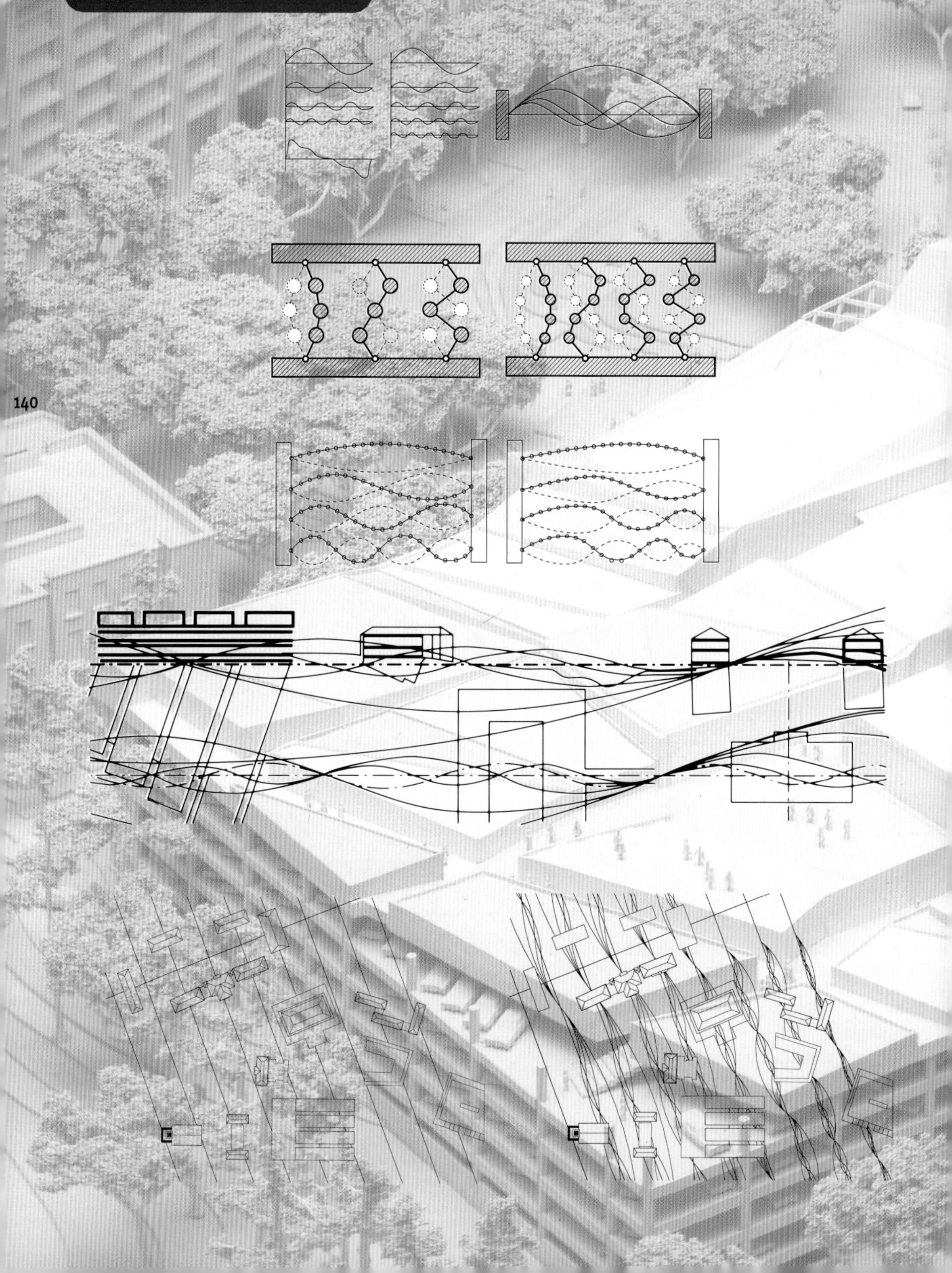

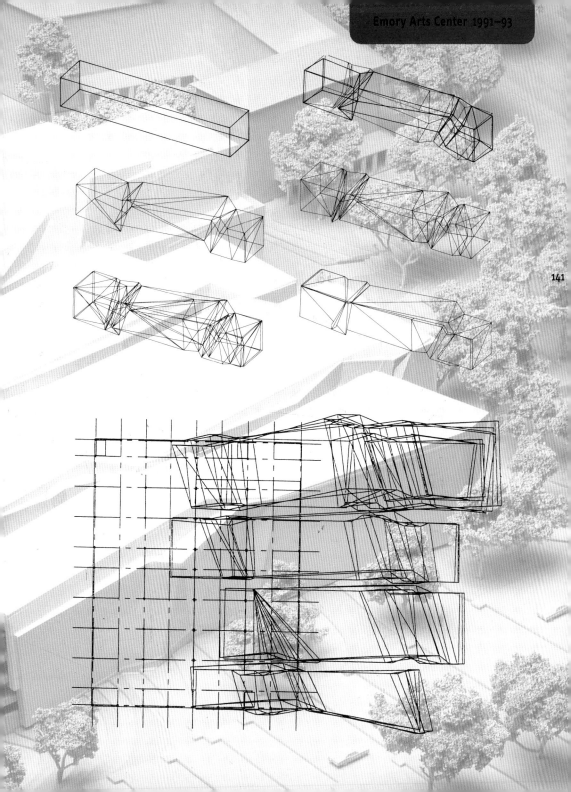

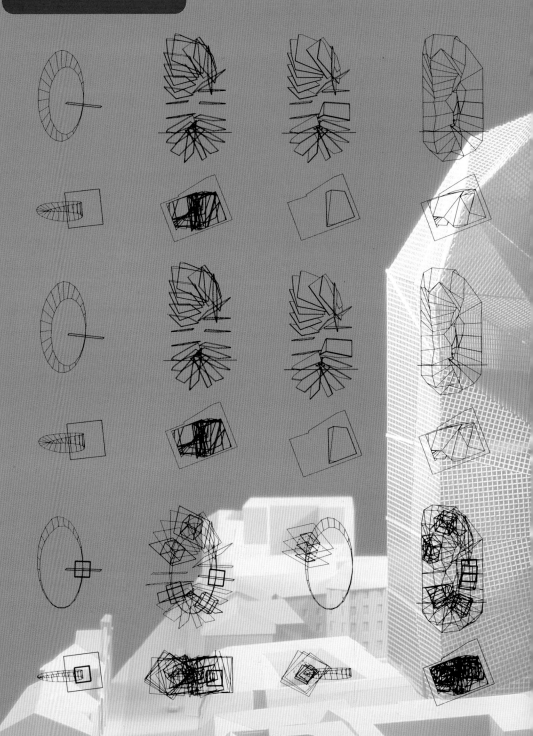

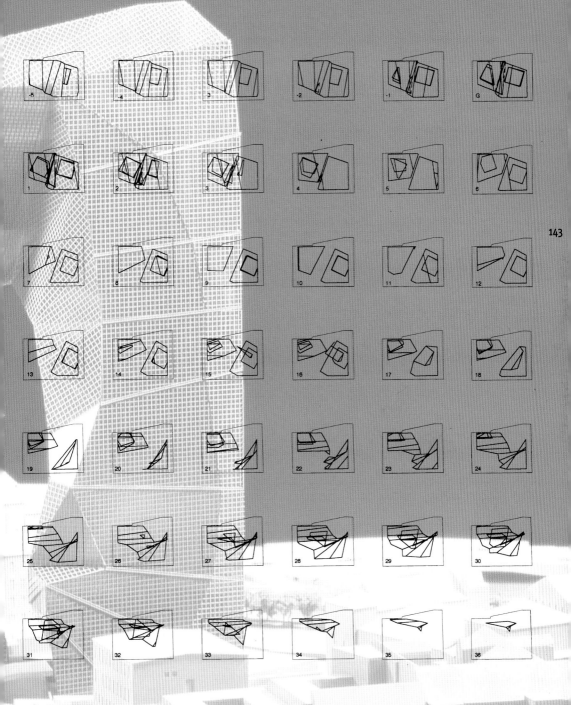

144

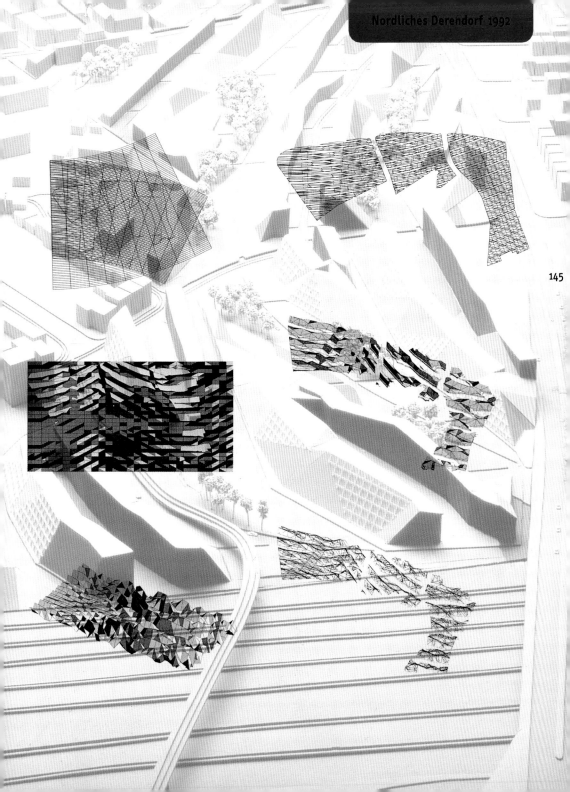

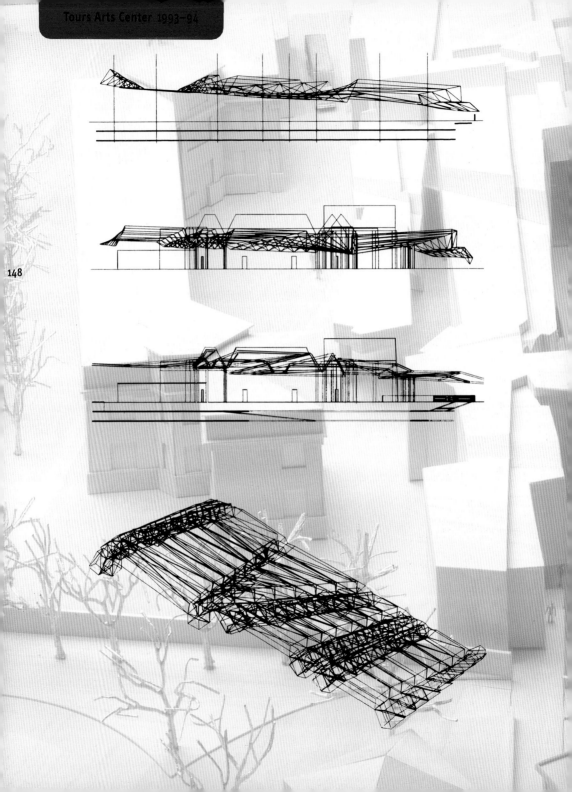

Klingelhöfer-Dreieck 1995

151

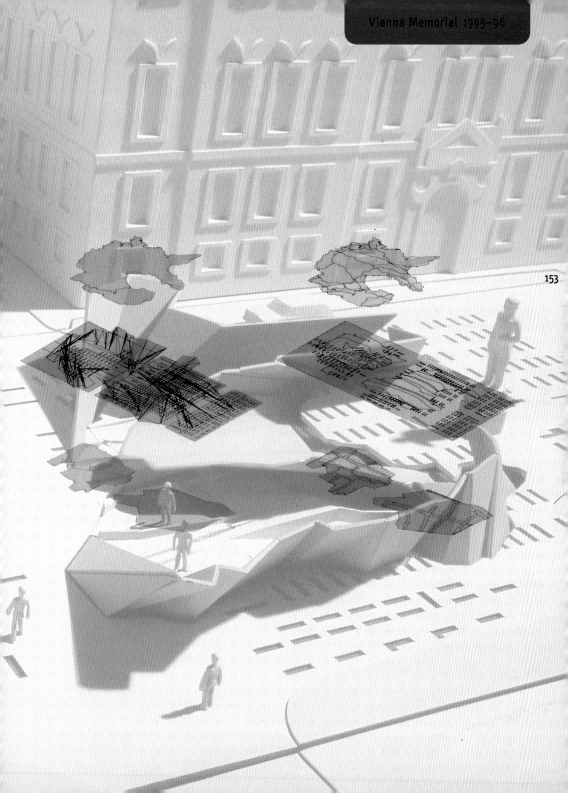

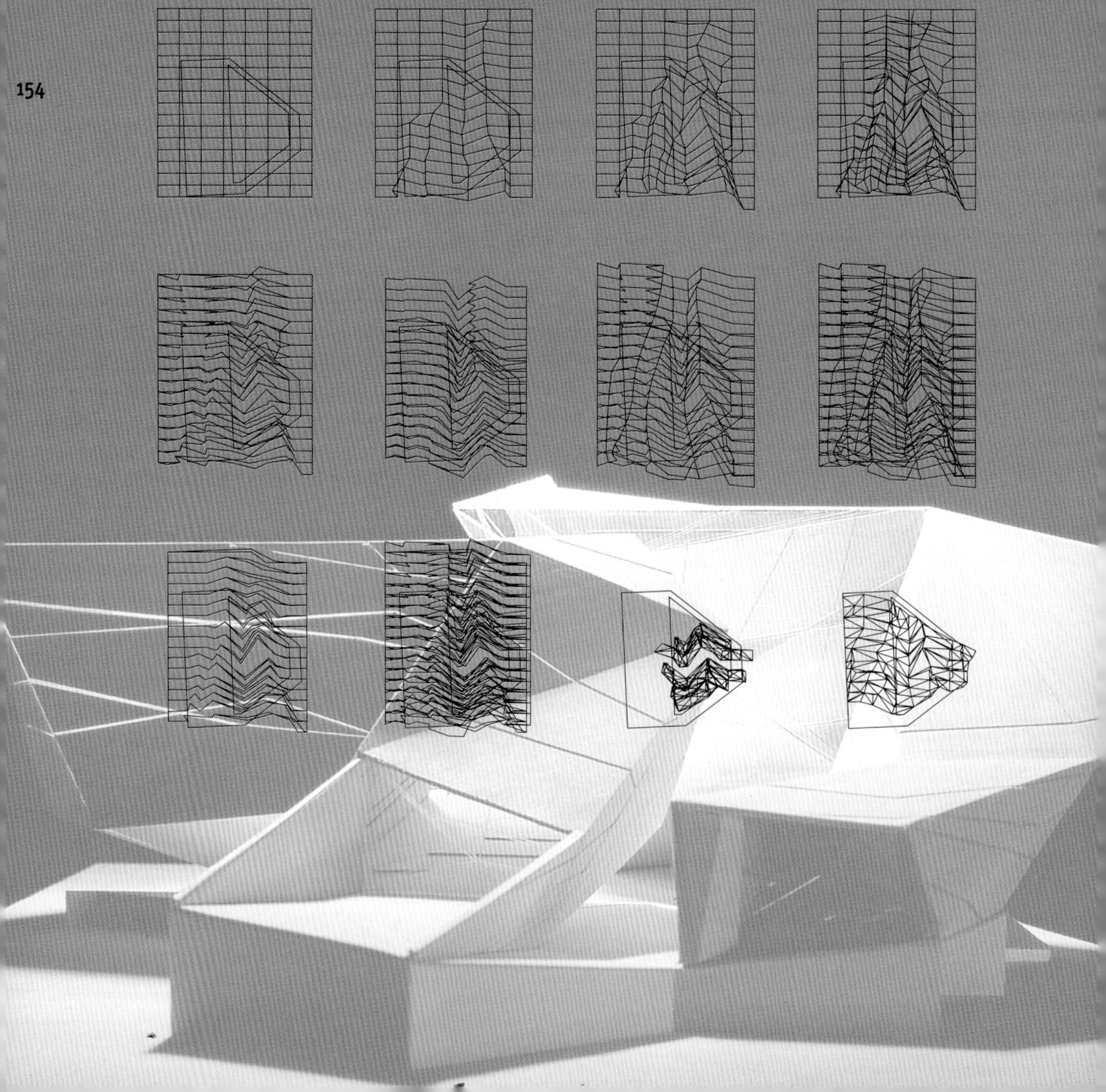

155

156

157

158

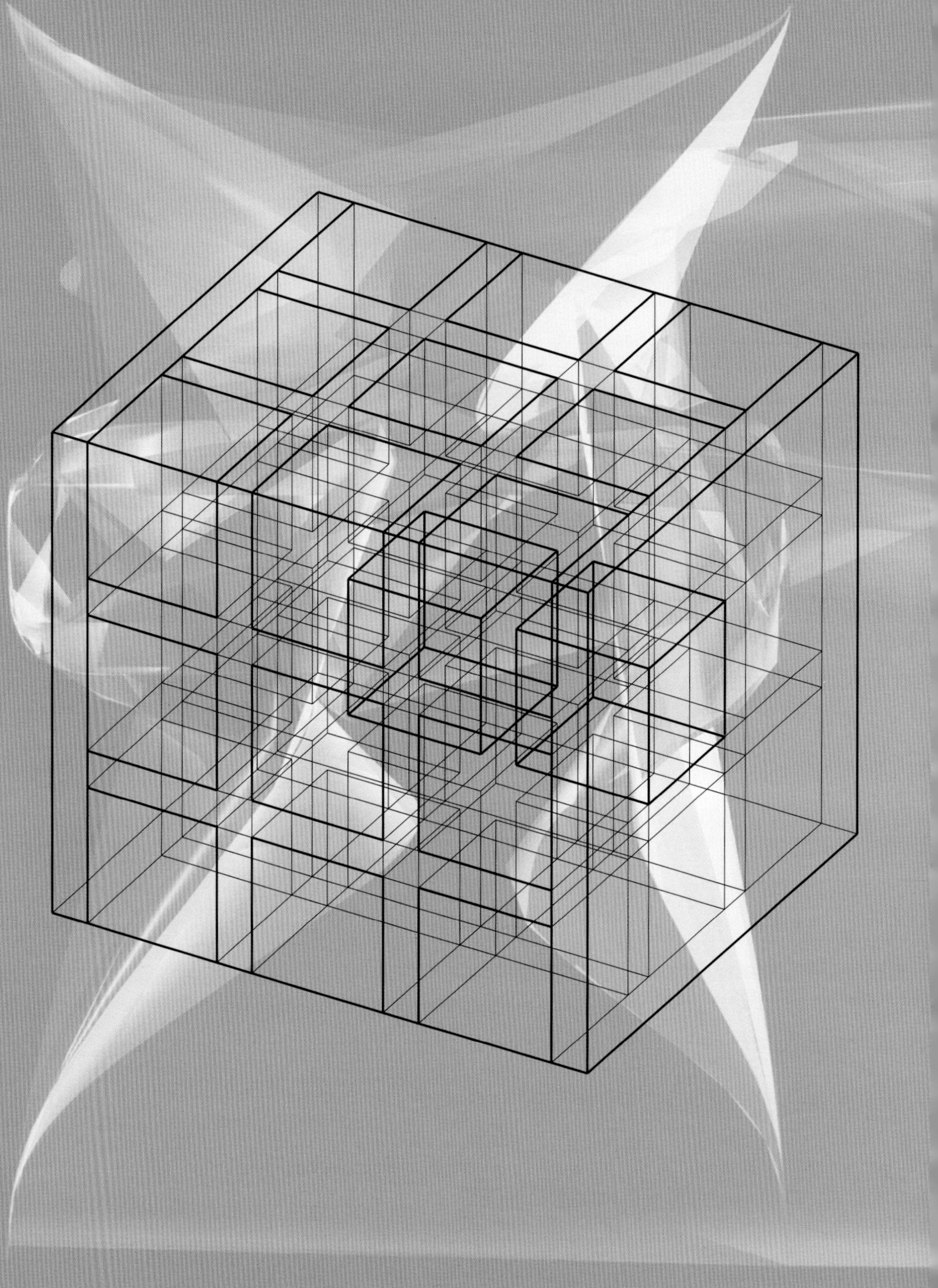

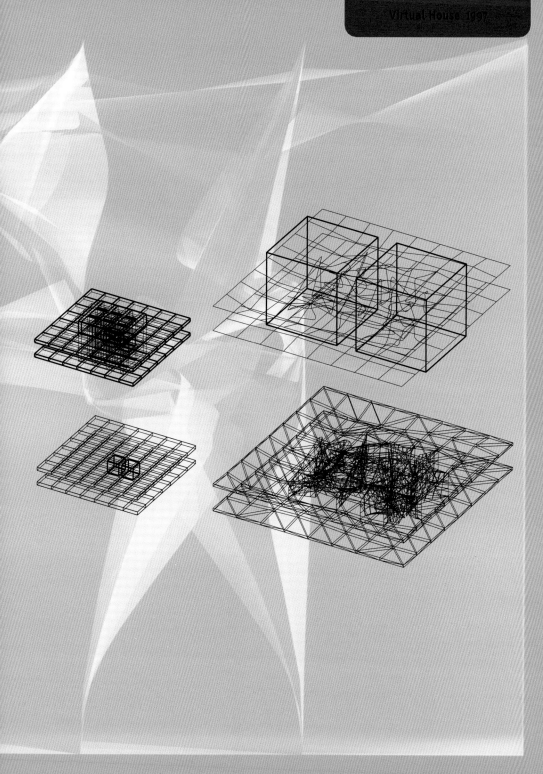

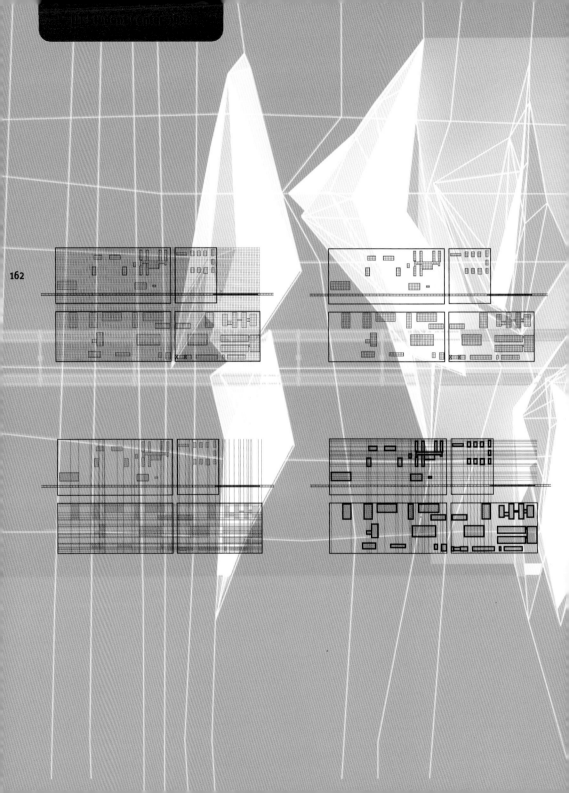

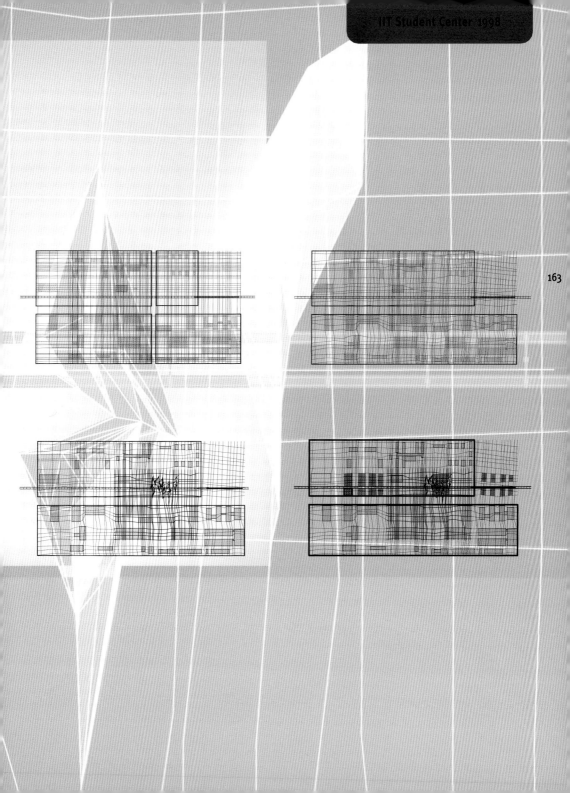

Diagrams of Exteriority
Peter Eisenman

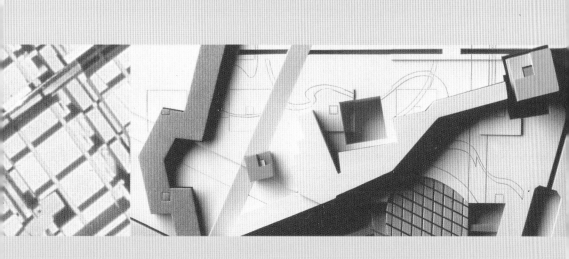

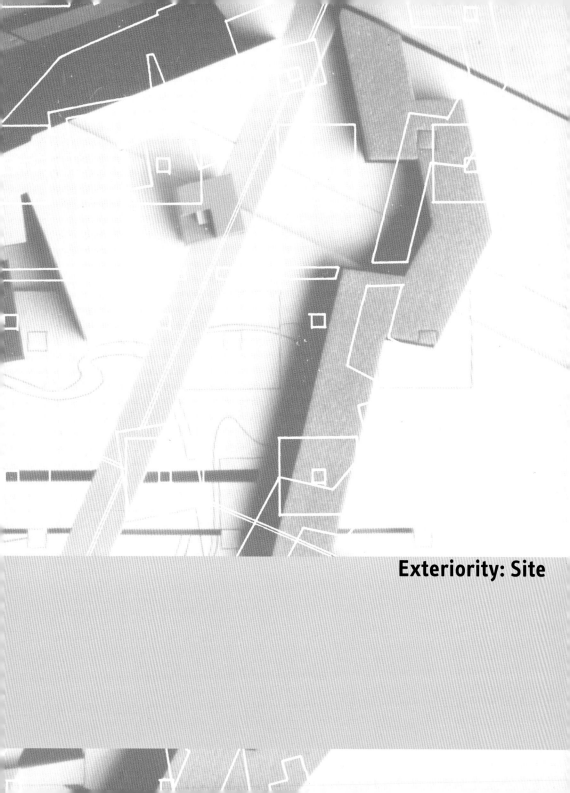

Exteriority: Site

Writing this narrative text of the diagramming process is a retrospective act. It takes a process that did not have an inner trajectory and forces it to obey such a narrative structure. The first diagrams in my Ph.D. thesis were never intended as the beginning of such a process. Rather, that work intended to distinguish my idea of the formal from other interpretations of the time. It proposed a relationship of built work to an interiority of architecture, something that seemed to be absent from other formal discourses. Most formal studies at that time concerned an analysis and explanation of buildings. My use of the diagram, therefore, was fairly innocent. It was a way of opening up the relationship between an interiority and individual buildings. As the idea of interiority began to develop in my own work, the diagram also became more implicated; it was not only explanatory but also generative. However, when the diagram became a generative device—when it was not merely used to

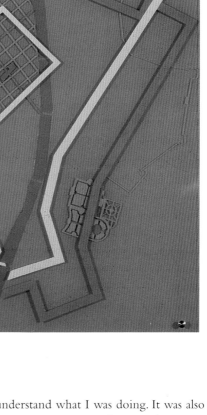

explain the relationship between a building and interiority—it introduced other concerns. It suggested an alternative relationship between the subject/author and the work. Such an alternative suggested a movement away from classical composition and personal expressionism toward a more autonomous process. Diagrams became a means to uncover something outside of my own authorial prejudices. In this sense, diagramming was potentially a more rational and quasi-objective means to understand what I was doing. It was also a means to move away from a subjective consciousness to an unconscious diagramming apparatus. Second, the process suggested that the built work could manifest the traces of the diagramming process as a means of relating built work to the interiority of its discourse.

As the diagrams progressed through the houses, two issues concerning interiority became clear: (1) the diagrams assumed that interiority was an *a priori* condition of value,

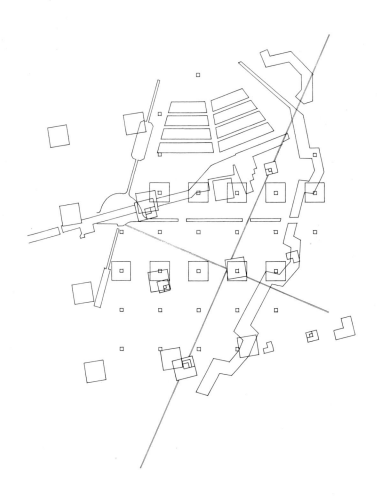

that is, a stable set of geometric icons, and (2) in transforming the geometry of the diagram into architecture, it was realized that geometry does not merely transform itself from a diagram to become architecture. Architecture is something more than geometry; walls have thickness, and space has density. Thus the value placed on any geometry—Euclidean or topological—as a prior condition of interiority would always be contingent on some architectural interiority. Thus, as the diagrams shifted from Euclidean to topo-

logical geometry, it was seen that this substitution of one geometry for another merely displaced the value given to Euclidean geometry without displacing geometry itself. This raised other questions: Why did the diagram necessarily evolve from some preexistent geometry? Why did the diagram begin from an architectural interiority that was not seen as a stable condition of essences? If interiority was unstable, was it possible that some other process other than transformation was appropriate to diagramming?

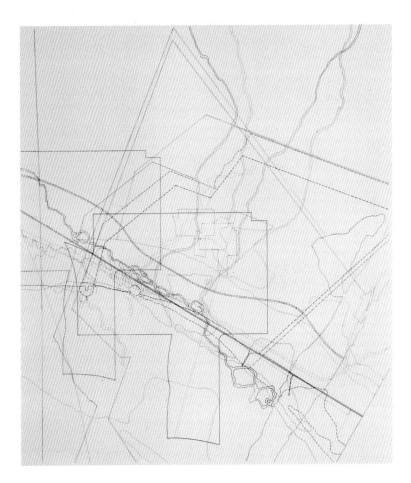

As an initial answer to these questions, the idea of a process of decomposition suggested that the interiority of architecture could be seen as a complex phenomenon from which a *less* complex condition of the object could be distilled. Interiority in this sense was no longer seen as either pure and stable or necessarily geometric. But because architecture is always based in geometry, the value of a formal universe as an embodiment of architecture was still present. In order to displace these embodied values, a series

of other diagrams was introduced into the diagrammatic process that were not based in geometry, which could be seen in some way to relate to, but at the same time be distanced from, an interiority as it had been previously defined. Thus, a series of external texts was introduced in an attempt to displace that which seemed embodied, immanent, and ultimately motivated in architecture's interiority.

These outside texts questioned the pervasive value given to anything embodied, or imma-

nent, in the interiority of architecture. If diagrams had to begin from such origins of value,
whether from inside or outside architecture,
they would always have an *a priori* embodiment—they would be motivated diagrams. At
the same time, the question was asked: could
such an embodiment ever be absent, without
abandoning the discourse? Thus the idea of
seemingly random and arbitrary texts from
outside architecture was introduced in an
attempt to overcome the immanence of architectural embodiment or the motivation of its
signs. While there is no such thing as arbitrary—there is always some contingency—the
diagrams began to look for the contingent
structures in the arbitrary, structures which
when inserted into real three-dimensional
space would produce alternative conditions of
the figural such as the interstitial, the affective,
and the blurred, conditions which could open
up the existing rhetoric and tropes sedimented
in architecture's anteriority.

The Cannaregio housing project in Venice was the first project to use what might be called an external text in that it is the first of six projects to consider site as an exteriority. Cannaregio was also the first project that used site as a conceptual datum. This corresponded with my psychological work at the time, which was attempting to move my psychological center from thinking to feeling, from the head to the body or to the ground. The project itself bracketed the project for House 11a in time, and House 11a itself traced back into Cannaregio. Cannaregio was the first project to be called by its "real" name, and significantly, its dominant reference was the first which was external to interiority in that its concerns were primarily site-related. It also introduced a mathematical figure, the Möbius strip, which will continue to be explored in later projects as a principal architectural figure.

The Cannaregio project asked the following question: If interiority was no longer stable, then could the ground, an assumed architectural

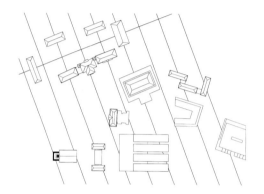 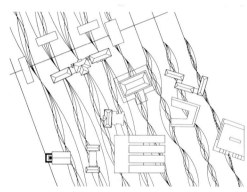

datum, also be questioned? This questioning of the ground datum would be the basis of many of the following projects. At Cannaregio, the surface of the ground was conceptualized as artificial, no longer a Euclidean datum but rather as a topological surface. In this context, any geometric form, whether Euclidean or topological, was seen to be artificial—that is, without any original value. A diagonal cut visually connecting the two major bridges on the periphery of the site was made in the surface,

both to mark it as a surface and to mark the topological axis. It is interesting in this context that the axis became a cut rather than a pedestrian connection. Along the cut, the site was turned up like a rubber sheet to articulate the idea of it as a surface as opposed to a ground. The site diagrams developed as an extension of Le Corbusier's grid for his Venice Hospital project, which had a series of nodes as places of exchange. This point-grid was extended to the project site and the nodes were inscribed as a

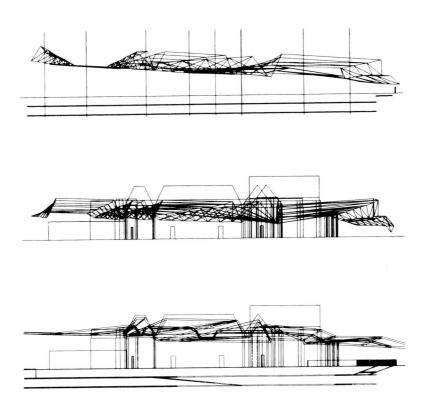

gridded matrix of voids in the topological surface. The Euclidean grid was now imprinted
into a topological surface, confounding any idea
of either Euclidean or topological geometry as
an originary or base condition.

Kurt Forster, who was teaching at Stanford
University at the time, was interested in the
conceptual intentions of the Cannaregio project and asked me to do a house for him on a
site he had in California. He described the
house he wanted in psychological terms. He
said, "I want a house that when I am inside I
feel like I am looking at the world from the
outside, and when I am outside the house it is
as if I am inside the house." This became the
program for House 11a. It contained in its
largest, most "inside" space an "inaccessible
void." It was a room with no doors and no
windows and thus no access. Therefore, the
most inside part of the house was conceptually
the most outside, because it could not be
entered. The subject could walk in and around

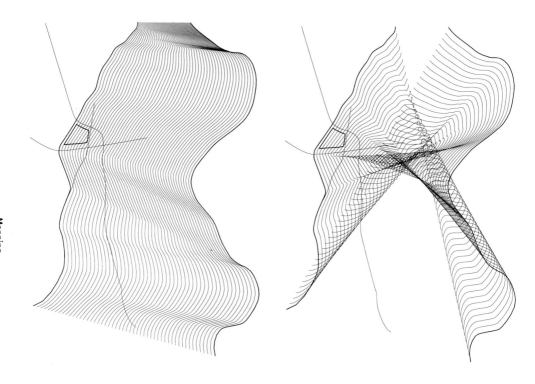

the house, up and down, but it was not possible to enter this large "inaccessible void." This inside/outside theme then suggested another external text as an initiating diagram for the house, that of a Möbius strip.

The Möbius strip is a topological surface that when twisted through itself is both continuous and denies the notation inside and outside; each side is alternately inside and outside. Diagrammatically, House 11a was conceptualized as a Möbius strip that would

be placed half underground and half above ground. The half which was underground became the living quarters, and the half which was above ground contained the inaccessible void. In this context, "under" and "above" ground became equated with "inside" and "outside" ground.

From the work on House 11a, the Cannaregio project was reconsidered and scaled versions of the house were placed in the matrix of voids. There were three differ-

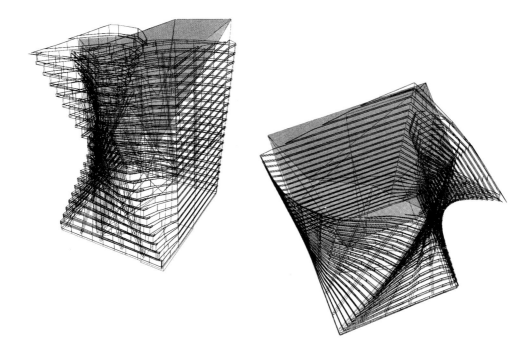

ent scales of the house which called into question the idea of the naming of "house." Each scale was nested inside the next largest scale, like a series of Russian dolls. The smallest scale was a model of House 11a. The next scale was the size of the house, with the model nested within it. It was no longer a house but a museum that contained the model of a house. The next scale was larger than the house, and had nested within it both the house and the model. Was it then a muse-

um of houses? These three different scales made it impossible to say which was the appropriate, or real, scale. It was also impossible to name the objects and thus relate form to function.

The first project dealing with explicit diagrams of artificial excavation was the competition for the office and housing complex at Berlin IBA Housing in what was then West Berlin. Following from Cannaregio, it again concerned the idea of a fictional ground. The

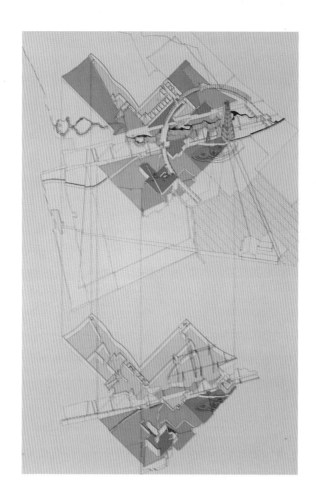

term "The City of Artificial Excavation" was used because the project invented a fictional, artificial Berlin, using three superposed grids. The diagrams mapped a series of ground inventions for a history of the site, using a process of superposition. *Superposition* is different from *superimposition*, in that it proposes no originating ground; figure and ground are interchangeable integers. The site at Berlin IBA Housing was next to a three-meter-high section of the Berlin Wall. The project walls

became a ground of the same height, thereby erasing the wall as a barrier and suggesting that the new ground of Berlin would be at a height of three meters. In positioning the site walls, the diagrams consisted of three superposed grids: a modern grid of squares; the eighteenth-century Berlin street grid; and an abstract Mercator Grid. The site of the Berlin IBA Housing project was the junction between the eighteenth-century perimeter blocks—where the blocks are the solid figures

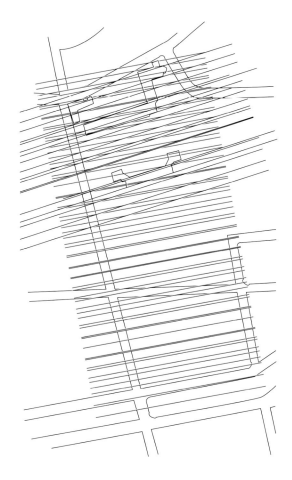

and the streets are the leftover void ground—
and the nineteenth-century avenues, where
the street-voids become the figures. From this
idea, the traditional figure-ground notation
was reversed and the ground was figured. A
topological axis was placed diagonally, tipping
the ground plane through the three grids. The
residual el-shaped pieces were tipped out of
the ground to form the buildings, leaving
imprints of these grids both on the ground
and on the buildings.

The Wexner Center (1981–85) represented
another change in the process of diagramming
if only because the project presented a series
of complex internal functions that complicat-
ed any purely formal diagram. The diagrams
also considered site as a fictional narrative. It
was the second of the series of site projects
that dealt with artificial excavation, that is, the
invention of a site diagrammatically. In addition, it was the first project to use scaling as a
dominant process in the diagrams. Scaling

here involved the superposition of maps of
different scales in order to find a common
registration point, so as to uncover possible
figuration and thus hidden meanings that
might be latent in the maps.

The diagrams constructed a relationship
between the grid of the site and the grid of
Ohio. This grid was established in the early
nineteenth century when Thomas Jefferson
sent Lewis and Clark out to survey what
would become the Northwest Territory. Lewis

and Clark and the Virginia Land Company
surveyed from the south to the north while
surveyors from the Western Reserve of
Connecticut surveyed from the north to the
south. The surveys met at a line in Ohio, but
because the surveyors' transits were set with
different readings of true north, their grids did
not align. The imaginary line where the two
grids abut, called the Miami Trace, can be
experienced on many north-south roads that
line Ohio's counties. There is a point where

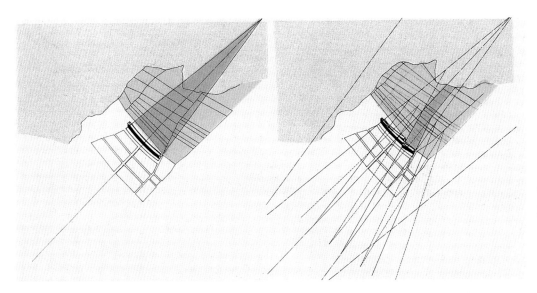

the roads turn ninety degrees in an east-west direction for some distance and then turn another ninety degrees back to north-south. In the design of the Wexner Center, this grid shift was scaled to our site and the building became a microcosm of the trace in the shifted grid. A second shift was provoked by Frederick Law Olmsted, who laid out a plan for the campus of Ohio State University. In order to make the campus a sanctuary from the Columbus grid— a separation of town and gown—Olmsted took

the grid of Columbus and shifted the axis of the main campus oval arbitrarily at 12.25 degrees. In order to unite the campus with the town grid, both grids were overlaid. Clearly the point of registration was critical to the resultant figuration. The diagrams were shifted over one another until a new reading appeared. These registrations generated the plan of the Center. Another site investigation found that the east-west runway of the Columbus airport and the axis of the Ohio State campus, tangent to the end of Ohio stadium, were all on the same 12.25-degree line. A conceptual axis could be drawn from the airport along the central axis of the campus to the closed end of the stadium. This line became the axis of entry into the building.

In one way or another, the diagrams of Cannaregio, Berlin IBA Housing, and Wexner all dealt with excavations and inventions of the site to provoke new readings. The problem with these diagrams is that they were essentially two-dimensional constructs, which in most cases only allowed for an extrusion into the third dimension for the built form. The three projects which followed—Romeo and Juliet, Long Beach, and La Villette—completed the series of artificial excavations. They attempted a different projection of the third dimension from diagrams of site. These three projects differ from the first three in that they introduced texts that were not immanent to either site or to an architectural discourse.

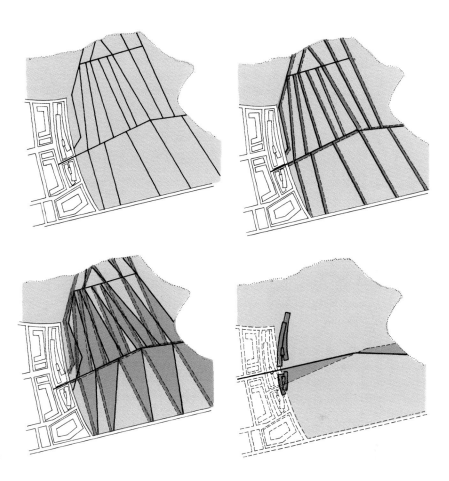

While the previous diagrams had initially been embodied with architectural significance—grids, axes, etc.—the diagrams which followed attempted to overcome this embodiment. This immanence made it difficult to blur any visual or conceptual relationship between form and function, since such a relationship was already inherent in the existing interiority. Thus the idea to introduce supposedly arbitrary texts that would no longer begin from any immanent architectural significance was proposed. Using such outside texts, artificial constructs were made (hence the term "artificial excavation"), using a process of superposition. These superpositions at different scales were then registered on crucial points to determine what kinds of overlaps, strange disjunctions, arbitrary figures, and ultimately new meanings could be produced. The intention was to produce figuration without conscious motivation—that is, figuration lying repressed within any text

Exteriority: Texts

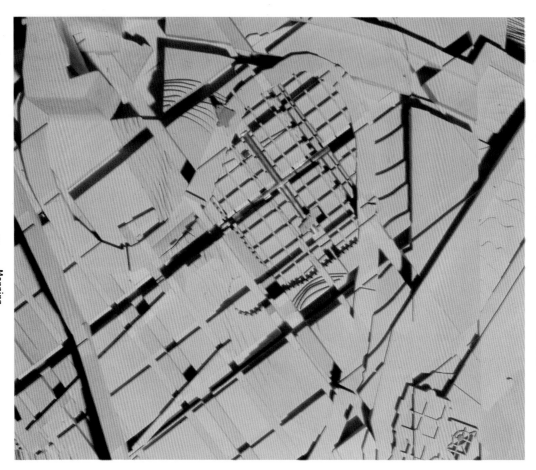

which might be opened up to new interpretations. Clearly the problem for such an approach was the reduction of architectural rhetoric—the tropes of anteriority—to a similar status as that of functional bubble diagrams.

The Romeo and Juliet project was done for Aldo Rossi's Venice Biennale in 1986. This was the first project to use an "outside" literary or scientific text other than site histories or mathematical figures. The idea of an outside text was chosen so that a series of dia-

grammatic figurations could be extrapolated from the texts which when registered and superposed over one another not only would obscure previous meaningful figurations, but more importantly would reveal other possible alternative, latent figurations. The given site was the site of the remains of what are called the Romeo and Juliet castles, visible from the autostrada between Verona and Vicenza. One is designated "Romeo's Castle" while the other is "Juliet's Castle," but they are unrelated

outside of this naming to the fictional Romeo and Juliet story. There are three different versions of this story, of which Shakespeare's is the third and last. While Romeo and Juliet appear as stable characters in each version, what happens to them varies. These fictions carry over to actual sites: In Verona one can visit Juliet's house, Romeo's house, and Juliet's grave. History has invented these "real" sites from a fictional origin. The process began with the superposition of Romeo's house in Verona on the site of Romeo's castle and Juliet's house on the site of Juliet's castle. This necessitated a change of scales in order to achieve a registration. The diagrams were presented on transparent sheets so as to be able to record different figurations depending on how they were registered. The three different scales of the diagrams, one for each version of the story, were each registered on three different points. The superposition produced new narratives in which something different from

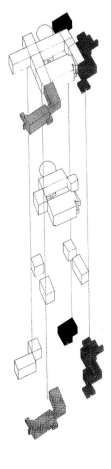

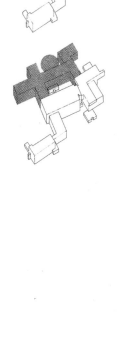

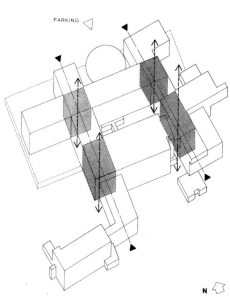

the given versions of the story could be read. The three resulting figurations were each modeled at different scales, presenting further narratives to be read.

The diagrams for the Frankfurt Biocentrum (1985), a new biology building for the Goethe University in Frankfurt, are a deviation from the Romeo and Juliet project, using a different textual strategy. While the Romeo and Juliet texts were immanent to the content and context of the given site, they were not immanent

to the program of the architecture. When the diagram comes from outside, there is a shift from a formal index to a written one. In the Biocentrum, however, the texts were not totally random, in that they were both immanent to the function of the particular building and also, in their indexical content, it was known that they would produce a geometry that could not be recognized as originating in function. These forms developed from the way in which scientists describe DNA chains, not

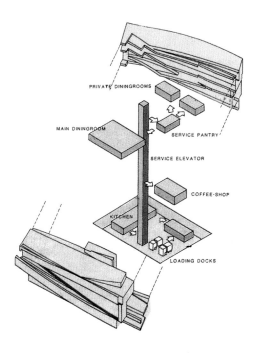

PRIVATE DININGROOMS

MAIN DININGROOM

SERVICE PANTRY

SERVICE ELEVATOR

COFFEE-SHOP

KITCHEN

LOADING DOCKS

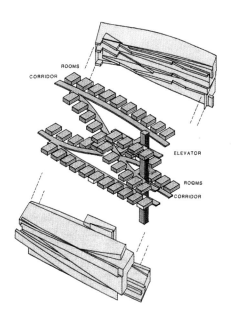

ROOMS

CORRIDOR

ELEVATOR

ROOMS

CORRIDOR

literally the double-helix diagram, but rather the forms of the scientific indices. The nucleotide chain became the base diagram for the site plan. The diagram of the building used the DNA chain for protein, which is composed of two toothlike forms with a fish tail on one end and a rounded end on the other. The individual forms in the chain are always differentiated and do not repeat; thus the chain structure is created by a repetition of difference. The specific forms of the building

were then extruded out of these chains. They were given a color notation of red-blue and light blue-brown, the same notation that the scientists use, reiterating the immanence of diagram and its function in the actual building project. In both Romeo and Juliet and the Frankfurt Biocentrum, the texts used to create the diagrams were seen to be immanent in the form and meaning of the buildings.

The diagrams for the Long Beach University Art Museum (1987), following from Romeo

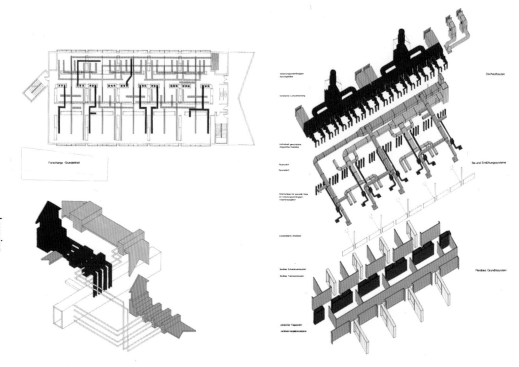

and Juliet, used a similar process of a superposition of texts. In this case, as in the Berlin IBA Housing project, these texts were historical maps of the site taken at different scales. These maps concerned three important dates in the life of the institution: 1849, the time of the gold rush; 1949, when the university was founded; and 2049, the upcoming one-hundred-year anniversary of the institution. The conceptual strategy was to produce a building that was to be found as a ruin in 2049, uncov-

ered two hundred years after the gold rush. The discoverers would find the traces of the maps recorded in the building form like a palimpsest of the history of the site. In the previous projects, which employed very elaborate layers in two dimensions, grids and figures were superposed and registered at different scales and then extruded into the third dimension. But these projects lacked an articulated third dimension. Long Beach was the first to attempt to have a non-extruded third dimen-

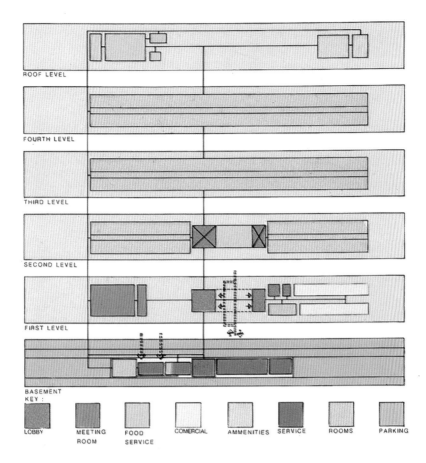

ROOF LEVEL

FOURTH LEVEL

THIRD LEVEL

SECOND LEVEL

FIRST LEVEL

BASEMENT

KEY :

| LOBBY | MEETING ROOM | FOOD SERVICE | COMERCIAL | AMMENITIES | SERVICE | ROOMS | PARKING |

sion. Therefore the way it was figured became an important part of the diagrammatic process. The superposition of the various traces were no longer registered over one another to produce a vertical third dimension. Rather the diagrams were shifted slightly to produce a warped third dimension.

Two projects, La Villette (1987) and Casa Guardiola (1988), began from supposedly arbitrary texts which were actually, in these two projects, *internal* to architecture. La

Villette, which was a collaboration with Jacques Derrida, used his text on Plato's *Chora* as a basis for an evolving idea of imprinting surfaces. The project began from an arbitrary set of diagrams—those of the Cannaregio project. This was because of an initial correspondence between Cannaregio and La Villette—both had once been the sites of slaughterhouses. The site conditions of Cannaregio were first superposed onto La Villette, producing an amalgam of the two. In

Exteriority: Mathematics

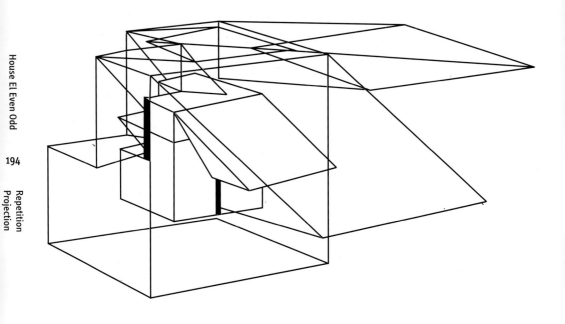

the process, Cannaregio was seen as a mold or Chora which was overprinted and then pulled away so that on the underside of the surface of the overprinting device, there would be the traces of this double work. Finally, the object that was imprinted would have similar marks on its surface, the trace of the activity of this process.

The diagrams of Casa Guardiola elaborated the work of trace and imprint begun at La Villette. The project used the diagrams of House X as an initial text. While this was an arbitrary decision, it provided a contingent if not immanent relationship to an architectural interiority since it related to both a prior project and thus to a form of anteriority, and also to certain tropes which define any architectural interiority. Casa Guardiola proposed a further development of the diagrammatic trace that would eventually lead to ideas of interstitial and folded space. The house suggested two distinctions: first, between geome-

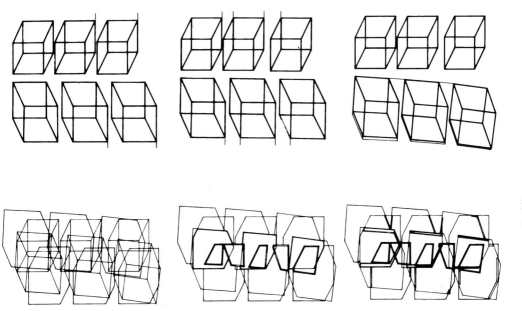

try and the tropes of architecture; and second, between tropes which are manifest by the fullness of presence and what could be called a between condition that was neither full presence nor total absence. In the La Villette project, absences were marked as imprints; again, an object was pushed into a mold, and when it was taken away, it left an imprint in the mold. In Casa Guardiola the idea of trace was introduced, which was seen as conceptually different from an imprint. The difference

was similar to what happens when you put your foot in sand on the beach. The foot makes an imprint in the sand, but when the foot is lifted up, sand crystals remain on the toe, instep, and heel of the foot—not in any kind of formed way but as a fragmentary trace of the step imprint. The trace is the random condition of the sand displaced by the foot which remains on the foot.

Thus two of the volumes of House X acted like the foot or imprinting mechanism for

Casa Guardiola. The volumes were placed into a negative mold of the same volumes of House X, which acted like the sand. When the positive volume was pulled away, imprints appeared on the mold, while partial traces were left on the volume. Since the volumes did not fit perfectly into the mold, there was a space between the volumes and the mold. The resulting space bore both traces and imprints from the volumes and the mold. This was the first use of an interstitial space as a

trope of interiority. Here, the interstitial was no longer understood as the traditional idea of solid poché, but rather as a space between spaces, articulated only by marks, traces, and imprints of its defining conditions.

After several projects working with super-position and registration, it was realized that while these projects dealt with the surface of the ground, none of them dealt with the edge of the intervention—how the new site dealt with the old. In the Frankfurt Rebstockpark master plan, that edge became a defining issue. The intention was to blur the distinction between old and new, to produce a seamless transition from old to new. This led to two new diagrammatic operations—one concerned the graft and the other the fold.

Graft is an operation similar to but different from collage. Whereas collage brings things from disparate contexts together in a new context, the juxtapositions—the edges—are necessarily articulated. The disjunctions of meaning rely on the fragmentation and the alien nature of the pieces to one another and to the whole. Graft, on the other hand, is more like montage, in that it involves time. Like the jump-cut in film, which makes seamless connections between events which are out of sequence, the graft also attempts to make a seamless connection between the new and the old. It attempts to erase the boundary or the frame of that which has been added in order to make the new project an amalgam of

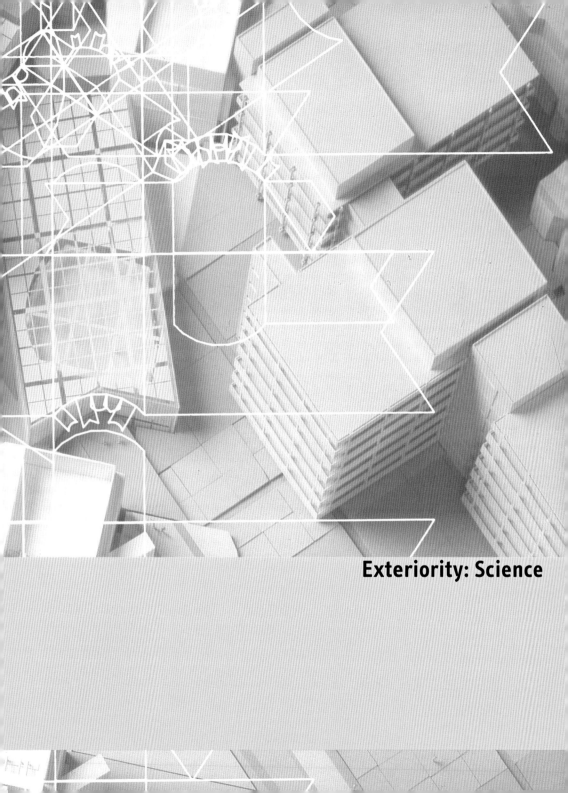

Exteriority: Science

old and new. Such a graft was the basis of the Rebstockpark project; it was accomplished through the agency of the fold.

Folding is different from superposition in that superposition preserves the simultaneity of figure and ground, whereas folding provides for a groundless, smooth depth. Work on the fold originated from Rene Thom's catastrophe theory diagrams. As John Rajchman has said, "Rebstock is a smooth, folded space, rather than a striated, collaged one." For

example, in origami, folds only figure the folding; at Rebstockpark, the frame is also folded. Origami is linear and sequential and ultimately involves a frame, whereas the folding at Rebstock is nonlinear and simultaneous. The folded surface does not look like the old, yet attempts a smooth transition, a between figure, between old and new. The site became the articulation of all the repressed immanent conditions. It does not destroy what is existing but rather sets it off in a new

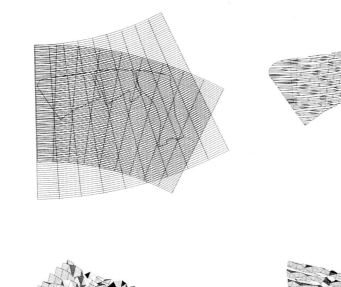

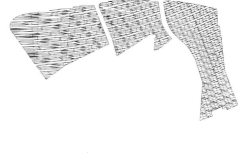

direction. In doing so, the fold gave to the edge a new dimension.

The idea of the edge as a smooth transition continued in the diagramming of the Tours Arts Center. This time, the blurring occurred in the figure itself rather than the ground through a process using computer morphing techniques. The morphing process took the two existing buildings which framed the site, one from the eighteenth century and one from the nineteenth century, and used them as boundary conditions. Just as it is possible to produce a figure between the letter A and the letter B which combines characteristics of both, so too did the Tours Arts Center become a between figure. It was made up of a series of layers which marked the transition from the eighteenth-century building and the nineteenth-century one. The diagrams of the morphing process became sectional templates which began to suggest conditions of interstitiality like those found in Casa Guardiola.

Exteriority: Science

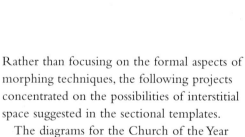

Rather than focusing on the formal aspects of morphing techniques, the following projects concentrated on the possibilities of interstitial space suggested in the sectional templates.

The diagrams for the Church of the Year 2000 (1996) and the Bibliothèque de L'IHUEI (1996–97) both began with the introduction of such an arbitrary text in an attempt to blur the iconic significance of the projects and also to produce interstitial space. It is in this sense that diagrams are contingent in that it is known *a priori* that they must yield spatial characteristics that both blur iconic forms and produce interstitial spatial possibilities. The idea was to limit the traditional iconic features of a church—bell tower, baptistry, etc.—specifically those forms that lead to recognition and thus meaning. The molecular diagrams of the liquid crystal were used for the spaces of the Church for the Year 2000. The object produced can be called a ground figure in that it evolves out of the ground,

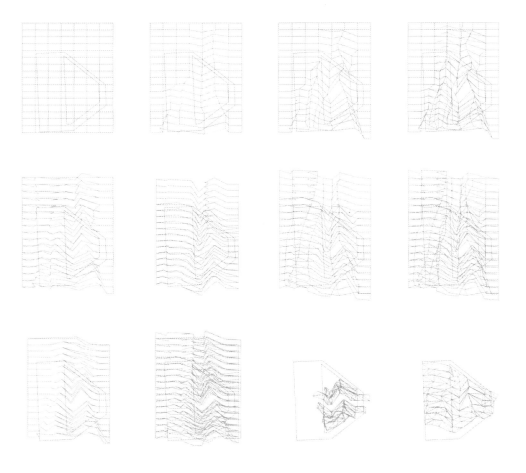

twists and warps in space, and returns back into the ground. It seems more like some convulsion of the ground rather than a building object on the ground. The diagram in this sense was contingent in that it produces a form that both iconically and functionally did not look like a church. That is, the initial image reading as church needed to be displaced and overcome.

The Bibliothèque de L'IHUEI, a library for the Place des Nations in Geneva, also began from an arbitrary yet contingent text. This was the diagram produced from the wave functioning of the human brain. In the Church for the Year 2000, the liquid crystal diagrams had some relationship to the liquid crystal television screens on the exterior of the church. The liquid crystal could therefore be seen to have some form of contingency which was not at the same time immanent in the architectural discourse. The diagrams for the library, however, did not have the same level of imma-

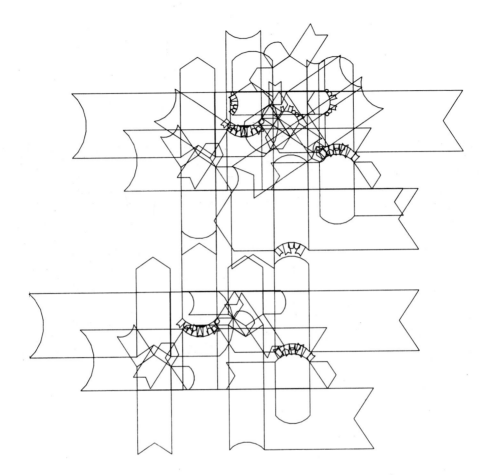

nent contingency. Instead, the diagrams, rather than their disciplinary origin, were important in that they led to a certain structure of operations. Again, the overcoming of the initial image was an important factor, but here the possibility of the diagrams to produce interstitial space was of equal importance.

The diagramming process in the Bibliothèque de L'IHUEI attempted to blur the direct relation between its form and its function through the idea of an interstitial spatial layer-

ing. Like the Church for the Year 2000, the diagrams proposed an image that no longer looked like a building, no less a library. The library, like the church, looked like it erupted from the ground. In previous projects, the diagrammatic process dealt with the idea of imprinting onto a hard surface. In the Bibliothèque de L'IHUEI, the imprinted surface was no longer conceptualized as hard but more like a balloon filled with sand. When a balloon is filled with air and then punched, it

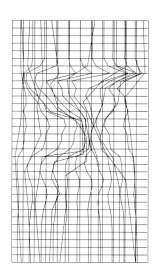 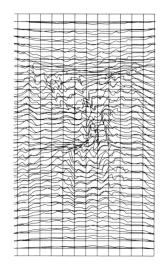 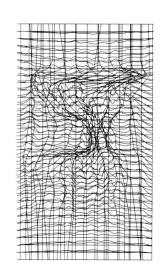

breaks. But when a balloon is filled with sand
or water and is then punched, it undulates
and pulsates. It moves from one place to
another, pushing in and out in a seemingly
random fashion. The imprinting process here
produced a pulsation that would allow the
form to record the varied pressures of in and
out movement. In this condition both the
space within the solid—the so-called interstitial space—and the solid itself were, in a
sense, seen as reactive in that they would

interpenetrate one another. One solid would
push in, and this would cause a reaction in
the other solid of pushing out. Whereas in the
Casa Guardiola project the process of trace
and imprint was static, here it was dynamic.
The idea of the interstitial in these diagrams
suggests that the container and the contained,
absence and presence, fullness and its lack, are
each affected simultaneously.

The diagram is a tactic within a critical
strategy—it attempts to situate a theoretical

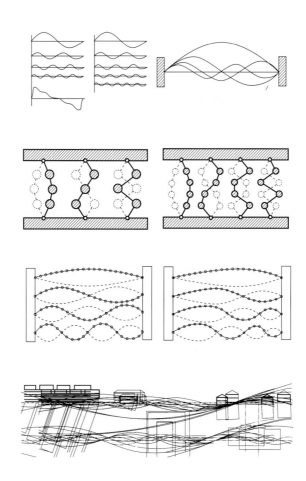

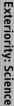

object within a physical object. It is the relationship between interiority and the theoretical object that is the critical content of the work displacing the functional, iconic, physical object of architecture. It is the embedded theoretical object which in a sense is the trace of the critical activity; it is this activity that becomes ideological.

All diagrams are both theoretical and ideological; they express an ideology about theory. The use of the diagram in a critical context has been recognized unconsciously by clients as an ideology. Ideology provokes a certain anxiety because it threatens the fundamental conditions of power; ideology deals with both super-structure and sub-structure, not as purely theoretical operations but as a critique of the relationship between them.

In order to practice critically an architect must develop, as the chameleon does, a form of camouflage, because clearly the motivation for all clients is some form of legitimation of

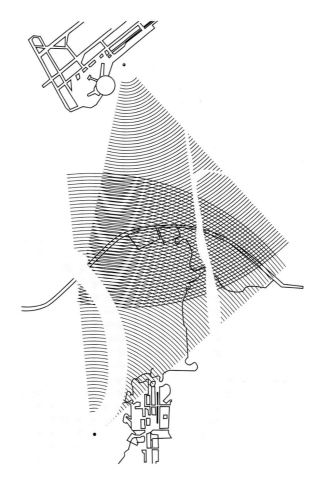

power. Architects can never directly attack this power, but rather can only displace it through some form of mediation. While it is possible to teach ideology and to theorize ideologically, I am not convinced that the work in an office can ever be in the same ideological vein. That is, I no longer feel compelled to insist upon an ideological sub-structure in my own work.

If one looks back on the work, historically, thirty years from now, will it be said that this loss of ideology was a late period, a playing out of an endgame? Or will it be said that this publication marks a new opening to something else, a freeing of the work from an ideological necessity? In one sense the diagram has reached a certain denouement in the work of the office. As an endgame it can now be theorized after so many years of the work. It seems ironic that only now, in the last few years, when the diagram seems to have had a theoretical rebirth, that our work of thirty years on the same sub-

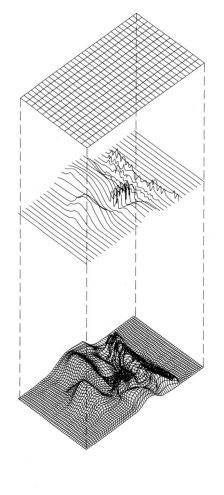

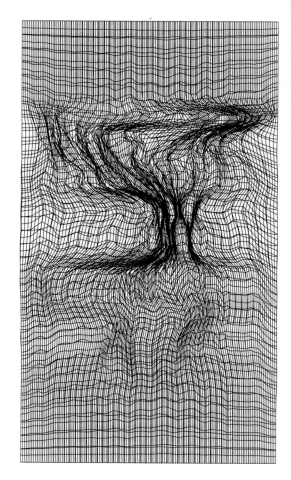

ject has become relevant. In one sense, this book stands as a critique of that rebirth, and in another sense, it is an acknowledgment that the larger the projects become, the less control that any architect has, no matter what the process. When politics and economics become the ruling factors, any critique—while perhaps more necessary—also becomes more problematic. Equally, in larger projects, it is not possible to displace function quite so easily. Therefore, if one cannot displace function, which is an ideo-

logical trope of the work, then the work itself must be reexamined.

Yet size is not the only factor that accounts for this change. The diagram has come full circle from the strategies of reading to the tactics of visceral experience. At the same time, the diagram seems to disappear from the built work. In projects such as the Virtual House, the Staten Island Institute, and the IIT student center, it becomes more or less a virtual entity, rather than being made explicit in

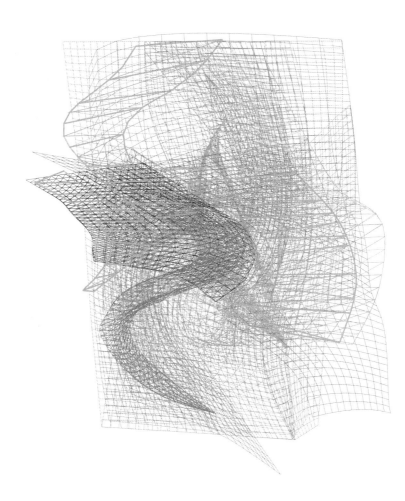

the projects. This is because the diagram becomes more of an engine in the projects rather than something which transforms itself into a physical reality.

The external diagram provided a series of formal relationships and organizations that when given form, structure, and function in an architectural context, did not permit these forms to be understood as coming from a known interiority—that is, a sedimented relationship between form and function. Lastly, and perhaps of equal importance, these diagrams shifted the focus of the reading strategy from its origin in formal relationships, and then linguistic and textual relationships, to the possibility of reading affective relationships in the somatic experience itself. This shift in the nature and use of the diagram has been critical in the evolution of the work. A critical analysis of these diagrams is crucial if one is to reexamine the work. This book, then, is a beginning of that process.

The Diagram and the Becoming Unmotivated of the Sign

Peter Eisenman

Charles Peirce defines two categories of sign: the indexical sign and the symbol or iconic sign. These are distinguished by what he calls their *motivation*. Indexical signs possess motivation in that they have a natural or intrinsic relationship between the sign and the signified. A symbol or iconic sign, on the other hand, is one where there is no direct link or motivation present between the sign and the signified; the relationship is artificial and external.

Architecture can be considered a motivated sign system because the sign and the signified are one and the same thing. In architecture, a structural element such as a column is both a real column and the sign of a column. In language, on the other hand, the word *apple* is the sign of a real apple, but the real apple is also the sign of something else, such as the "Big Apple" or the sign of temptation in the Garden of Eden. There is already a metaphoric and therefore representational condition in the object *apple* that reaches beyond the object itself. Thus the real apple has both a conventional relationship to the sign *apple* and also becomes a sign of this other metaphoric relationship. Unlike the real apple, which is removed from its sign, the physical *column* is simultaneously an object and the sign of the object. It is a more complex reality than the apple. Initially because the column is a sign of itself, it can be considered as an indexical sign in that it receives its motivation from an internal, prior condition—the interiority of its being. When looking at a column, a viewer is first of all not aware of this interiority. Nor is the typical viewer certain whether he or she is looking at the object *column* or the sign of that object. The ordinary viewer, for example, cannot assess the column's actual structuring value. But that same viewer can see whether something looks like, i.e., represents, such a structuring function. In this sense, the physical being of the column is motivated;

as a sign, it is motivated to present what it patently is—its structuring presence—and nothing else. Therefore in the discursive interiority of architecture, the column, the wall, the floor, and the ceiling can initially be considered motivated signifiers; that is, nothing more than what they are or what they look like they are. This idea of "looking-like" is a self-referential or indexical condition of the sign; it is the prime indicator of the motivated condition of such an architectural sign, and in its most primal internal condition, it does not refer and point to a signified other than itself.

In the traditional design process, the architect takes this primal abstract idea of, say, a column, and transforms it into another form of motivated system, one that is artificial and results from an external relationship of the column to some other recognizable form (the body, a tree, etc.). This external condition is introduced because of a desire on the part of the subject to have architecture be meaningful and to communicate—in other words, to produce a conventional or artificial set of signifiers from an abstract idea. For example, when a column becomes articulated, such as when it is made into a classical column, or when it is made of fine marble, or when it is made too large or too small for its function, a motivation is placed in the column outside of its structuring or internal motivation. Thus, when architects design, they take objects which are initially internally motivated and attempt to turn them into an artificial set of signifiers, a communicating language, as some form of external motivation. There are, therefore, two types of motivation—one internal and one external. Both are motivated differently—one by an internal logic and the other by an external desire.

The traditional use of the diagram in architecture has been to take the internal motivation and transform it into an external one. For example, when a nine-square diagram is abstracted from a Palladian villa and then transformed in the design process to produce a contemporary building, the initial step is a reduction of the external motivation of the villa to the internally motivated diagram. But then in the transformation of the diagram into a contemporary building, the process returns the motivation to where it began, to a real building. This was the case in the use of the nine-square diagrams in my first house projects. The diagram was no more than an intermediate state between two similarly motivated, but stylistically different, buildings. But it is possible to suggest that the diagram can be used in an entirely opposite way: to reverse the motivated process of design. In doing so, diagrammatic work poses the following questions: 1) Can the metaphysics of presence be opened up or displaced? Is there another way to think presence other than through fullness? 2) Is there a way to rethink the relationship between the sign and the signified as other than a motivated relationship? and 3) Is there a way to rethink the subject as other than a subject motivated by a desire to have architecture communicate a sense of place and ground?

Jacques Derrida's argument about the sign and presence becomes useful as a way of considering the first question. Derrida argues that there is already in the sign a condition which he calls the *transcendental signifier*. In Derrida's argument, a sign does not merely relate to a signified but relates to a larger system of meanings. These meanings transcend a particular sign, but at the same time they relate to an overriding need to communicate. In other words, there is an original idea marking any sign. There is also a desire on the part of the subject to have an object be understood, that is, to make available a motivation in the signifier. Thus each signifier not only carries a desire in the subject to signify but also carries in the specific signifier the need for its own motivation. Derrida says that these two issues are linked in the metaphysics of presence.

Architecture, when it has been compared to language, has been thought of as spoken—as an *architecture parlante*. Spoken language always implies the here and now, and thus the primacy of presence. Logocentrism thinks of speech as fullness, and, in turn, metaphysics assumes speech to be an originary condition. Derrida argues against these assumptions when he says that speech is not a fullness but already contains an absence in the form of a writing. In language, speech is an initial cause of motivation. A writing, on the other hand, is motivated by the subject's desire to make some sort of sense out of the possibility of utterance. Thus the idea of writing possibly exists in a prespeech and predesiring state. Therefore, if a diagram can write architecture or to act as a writing (that is, to

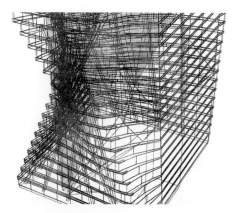

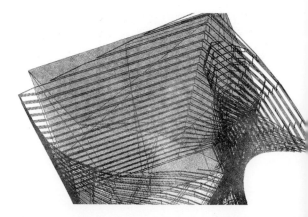

be written into a column or a wall), this writing could be something different from the column as having an explicit and external sign function. The idea of writing as a diagram is a means of potentially overcoming the question of origin (speech) as well as the metaphysics of presence. The diagram would be a means of reversing the motivated design process by insisting on its presence as a primary condition.

The necessity of any becoming in architecture has traditionally been the becoming of a presence. The diagram, in contrast to this, attempts to manifest a becoming-present of presence, which rather than changing from state A of presence to state B of presence, moves from a state of presence to non-presence, and in doing so, allows for the possibility of a non-presence within presence. In order to rethink presence, the diagram attempts to overcome the subject's initial desire for a communicating signifier. The diagram does this by producing a set of arbitrary connections to the signified by separating the motivated relationships between form and function, and form and meaning. These arbitrary connections would no longer be in the realm of the semiotic icon, but rather in a condition of an index. This removal and rupture allows a possible not-presence, a void within presence to be. This not-presence is a writing.

The diagram helps to displace presence by inserting a not-presence as a written trace—a sign of the not-presence of the column—into the physical column. This trace is something that cannot be explained either through function or meaning. For Derrida, the trace, which acts as a critique of the transcendental signifier, comes from an unconscious motivation, which causes it to appear in writing. This unconscious motivation comes from the arbitrary nature of the diagram. The trace belongs to the very moment of signification. In this context, traces can be considered one example of the mystical, since they cannot be understood within a structure of logocentrism as we know it or the metaphysics of presence. The intersection of the mystical and the rational operates when an arbitrary diagram which is inserted into the process acts to produce something in plan, section, or elevation, like the writing of the column.

Traditionally, artificial signs such as the classical column are thought to derive their motivation from a rational system of thought, from a logos based in the semiotic. While this may be so within Western metaphysics, Chinese characters, for example, are not only artificial or conventional signs; their forms come from another, more mystical system, a system which cannot be explained by a metaphysical relationship between logos (the sign) and the signified. While Chinese characters may carry a motivation, the signs are not con-

213

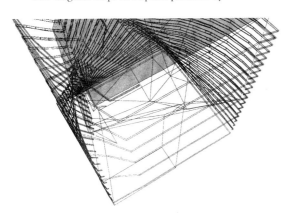
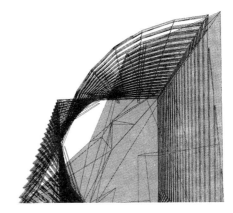

Haus Immendorff

understood by a traditional knowledge of how to read architecture. The diagram as a form of writing, because it introduces a not-presence as an absence in presence, presents the possibility of overcoming the idea of a motivated sign.

The idea of overcoming the motivated sign—the second question for the diagram—is a critical project for the diagram. Here, the diagram becomes an agent for the movement towards the becoming unmotivated of the architectural sign. But because of architecture's inherent motivated condition of sign, the diagram has a different function in architecture than it does in other disciplines. In order to act diagrammatically, the diagram must first overcome the motivated conditions that are at the root of architectural discourse. Equally, since architecture is a productive discourse in that it must structure, enclose, shelter, etc., these motivations can never be completely negated. What the diagram can do, however, is destabilize such motivated conditions as site, program, function, and meaning; in doing so, the diagram introduces the project of the negative.

This introduces the strategy of the diagram as a negative or resistant agent. In this context, the diagram begins to separate form from function, form from meaning, and architect from the process of design. The diagram works to blur the relationship between the desiring subject—the designer, the user—and the

desired object in order to move both subject and object towards an unmotivated condition. But at the same time, as Massimo Cacciari points out, it is problematic to act as a negative agent in architecture.

According to Cacciari, the negative as a realized or fulfilled nihilism is not possible in architecture because architecture is ultimately a productive discourse. This knowledge introduces into the negative a constant state of becoming, which, in turn, creates a nostalgia for completion.

Any such nostalgia ensures the persistence in architecture of a hierarchical language that in one sense overcomes the project of the diagram. The language of overcoming suggests a repression of that which is being overcome, and in that repression, produces a certain retrograde desire for its own fulfillment. While the diagram may succeed in unmotivating this desire for completion, since it can never achieve the fulfillment of the negative, the desire for fulfillment remains. The becoming unmotivated of the sign and the becoming unmotivated of the subject's desire marks the becoming unmotivated of the desire for completion as a *motivation*. The becoming unmotivated of the desire for fulfillment is not the same as the *loss* of desire for fulfillment. If the desire for fulfillment is lost, the desire to project and to critique is lost. The diagram is one tool for unmotivating and

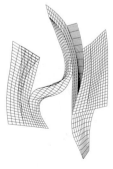
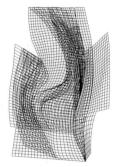

thus radically transforming the traditional desire for the possibility of completion. The diagram resides between the project and the author desiring fulfillment; it is an aporia projected as the impossibility of completion. In this sense, the diagram acts as an agent for the constant unmotivating of the desire for fulfillment.

Last is the question of the diagram in relationship to the subject's desire for ground or place. Derrida argues that the subject has a desire for place, for places—the house, the city, etc. This desire can be called an externally motivated desire. In this sense, place is not a neutral term. The diagram does not remove the desire for place but rather suggests that place could exist outside of such a motivation. This does not mean that there will no longer be a desiring subject but rather that these desires could come from a potentially unmotivated state. The diagram in this context attempts to place the subject into a desiring condition that is unmotivated by anything but an unconscious or less motivated desire. Such a less motivated condition of almost pure desire has no object, but rather only a trajectory. Place, therefore, should not be an objective, for when desire has an object, place is already motivated.

When these desires manifest themselves in the object of architecture, they do so as ground, place, and meaning. The diagram, through a continual deconstruction of presence, never arrives at a realization of either ground or no ground, but rather becomes a questioning of the project of presence which is ultimately grounded. At the same time, the diagram attempts to unmotivate place, to find within place space as a void, as a negativity or non-presence to be filled up with a new figuration of the sign. This new figuration is no longer within a semiotic system but is rather an index of affect, and, as affect, the void becomes a sign of not-presence, and thus the beginning of the transgression of the metaphysics of presence, which sees all signs as representing presence— and all presence as signs. Therefore, the notion of producing a sign of the not-presence in space begins to undermine presence and call into question the dominance of the fullness of the sign, and of the semiotic system itself.

Any possibility of a not-presence is always contingent upon a prior condition of presence. In other words, when place as a motivated sign is displaced, place becomes open to a void of space that can be filled again. And thus when the fullness of place is opened to a process of displacement, what remains is always a trace or a residue of place. The diagram as the potential for the voiding of place in space—the not-place in place becomes such a trace.

215

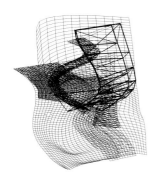
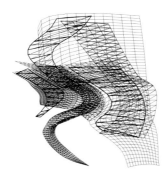
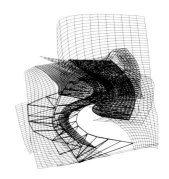

Appendix

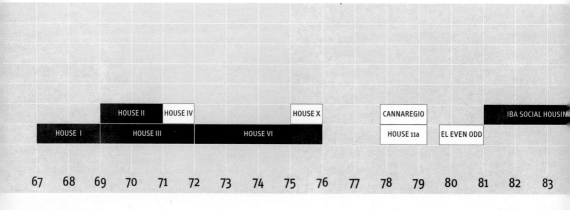

| HOUSE II | HOUSE IV | | HOUSE X | | CANNAREGIO | | | IBA SOCIAL HOUSING |
| HOUSE I | HOUSE III | HOUSE VI | | | HOUSE 11a | EL EVEN ODD | |

67   68   69   70   71   72   73   74   75   76   77   78   79   80   81   82   83

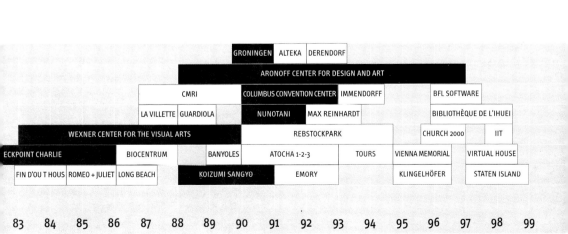

			GRONINGEN	ALTEKA	DERENDORF								

ARONOFF CENTER FOR DESIGN AND ART

CMRI | COLUMBUS CONVENTION CENTER | IMMENDORFF | | BFL SOFTWARE

LA VILLETTE | GUARDIOLA | NUNOTANI | MAX REINHARDT | BIBLIOTHÈQUE DE L'IHUEI

WEXNER CENTER FOR THE VISUAL ARTS | REBSTOCKPARK | CHURCH 2000 | IIT

ECKPOINT CHARLIE | BIOCENTRUM | BANYOLES | ATOCHA 1-2-3 | TOURS | VIENNA MEMORIAL | VIRTUAL HOUSE

FIN D'OU T HOUS | ROMEO + JULIET | LONG BEACH | KOIZUMI SANGYO | EMORY | KLINGELHÖFER | STATEN ISLAND

83   84   85   86   87   88   89   90   91   92   93   94   95   96   97   98   99

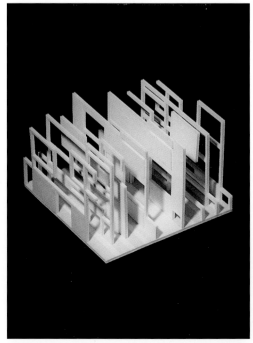

House I
Princeton, New Jersey: 1967–68

Architect: Peter Eisenman
Design Assistants: Russell Swanson, Robinson O. Brown
Drawings: Russell Swanson, Thomas Pritchard, Gregory A. Gale
Contractor: Bard Construction Co.

House II
Hardwick, Vermont: 1969–70

Architect: Peter Eisenman
Design Assistants: Russell Swanson, Gregory A. Gale, Robinson O. Brown
Drawings: Gregory A. Gale, Judith Turner, Christopher Chimera
Structural Engineer: Geiger-Berger
Contractor: Dutton Smith

House III
Lakeville, Connecticut: 1969–71

Architect: Peter Eisenman
Structural Engineer: Geiger-Berger
Mechanical Engineer: George Langer
Contractor: Joseph Maloney

House IV
Falls Village, Connecticut: 1972–76

Architect: Peter Eisenman
Design Assistant: Rodney Knox
Drawings: Ellen Cheng Koutsoftas

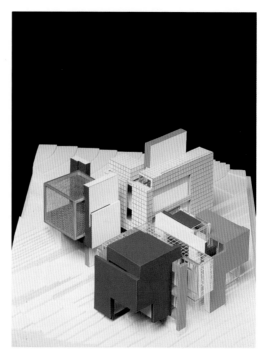

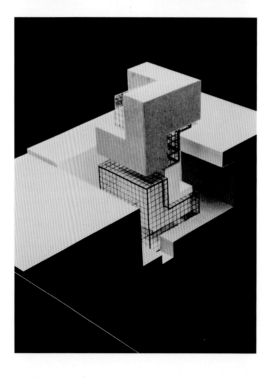

House VI
Cornwall, Connecticut: 1972–75

Architect: Peter Eisenman
Design Assistants: Randall Korman, Rodney Knox
Drawings: Read Ferguson, Caroline Sidnam, William Jackson
Model: Mark Mascheroni
Structural Engineer: Robert Silman & Associates
Contractors: Arthur B. Deacon & Sons, Robert Finney

House X
Bloomfield Hills, Michigan: 1975

Architect: Peter Eisenman
Associate Architect: Leland Taliaferro
Design Assistants: Mark Cigolle, Livio Dimitriu, John Nambu, Anthony Pergola, Noel Quesada
Structural Engineer: Robert Silman & Associates (Ding Carbonell)
Mechanical Engineer: Arthur Spaet & Associates (Arthur Fox)
Landscape: Nicholas Quennell
Cost: Stephen H. Falk
Model: Anthony Pergola
Axonometric Model: Sam Anderson

House 11a
Palo Alto, California: 1978

Client: Prof. Kurt Forster
Architect: Peter Eisenman
Project Team: David Buege, John Nambu, Joan Ockman
Models: Sam Anderson, Andrew Bartle

Cannaregio Town Square
Venice, Italy: 1978

Client: Municipal Government of Venice
Architect: Peter Eisenman
Project Team: David Buege, John Nambu, Joan Ockman
Models: Sam Anderson, Andrew Bartle

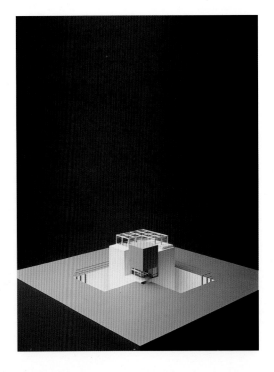

House El even Odd
1980

Architect: Peter Eisenman
Design Assistants: Mark Mascheroni, Caroline Hancock, Tom Howorth
Collages: Walter Chatham, David Buege, Cary Liu
Models: Tom Hut, John Leeper, Jim Uyeki, John Regan
Coordination: Eleanor Earle, Judy Geib
Structural Engineer: Robert Silman, Robert Silman Associates
Mechanical Engineer: Marvin Mass, Cosentini Associates

IBA Social Housing at Checkpoint Charlie
Berlin, West Germany: 1981–85

Client: Hauert Noack, GmbH & Company
Architect: Eisenman/Robertson Architects, New York; Groetzebach, Plessow & Ehlers, Berlin
Partners-in-Charge: Peter Eisenman, Dietmar Groetzebach, Gunther Plessow
Project Architects: Thomas Hut, Thomas Leeser, Wilfried Hartman
Project Team: Audrey Matlock, Doug Oliver, Frank Chirico
Drawings: Michelle Andrew
Models: Sam Anderson, John Leeper, Vera Marjanovic

Fin D'Ou T Hou S
1983

Architect: Eisenman/Robertson Architects
Partner-in-Charge: Peter Eisenman
Design Assistant: Pieter Versteegh
Drawings and Models: Bruce Dunning, Luis Feduchi, Pierre Jequier, Grazyna Mielech, Francois Poylo, Karl Van Suntum
Coordination: Ross Woolley
Preliminary Design: Katsuo Muramoto, Frank Chirico, Douglas Oliver

Wexner Center for the Visual Arts and Fine Arts Library
The Ohio State University, Columbus, Ohio: 1983–89

Partners-in-Charge: Peter Eisenman, Richard Trott
Directing Architects: George Kewin, Michael Burdey
Project Architects: Arthur Baker, Andrew Buchsbaum, Thomas Leeser, Richard Morris, James Rudy, Faruk Yorgancioglu
Project Team: Andrea Brown, Edward Carroll, Robert Choeff, David Clark, Chuck Crawford, Tim Decker, Ellen Dunham, John Durschinger, Frances Hsu, Wes Jones, Jim Linke, Michael McInturf, Hiroshi Maruyama, Mark Mascheroni, Alexis Moser, Harry Ours, Joe Rosa, Scott Sickeler, Madison Spencer, Mark Wamble
Consultants: Landscape Architect: Hanna Olin, Ltd., Laurie Olin, Partner-in-Charge; Structural Engineer: Lantz, Jones, & Nebraska, Inc., Tom Jones, Partner-in-Charge; Mechanical Engineer: H.A. Williams & Associates; Lighting Design: Jules Fisher & Paul Marantz, Inc.; Civil Engineer: C.F. Bird & P.J. Bull, Ltd.; Security and Fire: Chapman & Ducibella, Inc.; Graphics and Color: Robert Slutzky; Soils Engineer: Dunbar Geotechnical; Audio/Visual: Boyce Nemec; Acoustics: Jaffe Acoustics; Specifications: George Van Neil; Models: Scale Images, Albert Maloof, Gene Servini; Renderings: Brian Burr
Contractors: Dugan and Meyers, General Contractor, Jim Smith, Project Manager; A.T.F. Mechanical, Inc., Mechanical Contractor
Bob Weiland, Project Manager; Romanoff Electric, Electrical Contractor; Sib Goelz, Project Superintendent; Radico, Inc., Plumbing Contractor; Frank Czako, Project Manager; J.T. Edwards, Steel Subcontractor; Jack Edwards, President

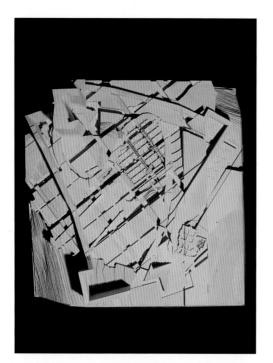

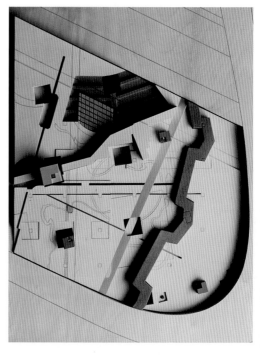

Moving Arrows, Eros, and Other Errors:
An Architecture of Absence (Romeo + Juliet Castles)
Third International Architectural Biennale
Venice, Italy: 1985

Architect: Eisenman/Robertson Architects
Partner-in-Charge: Peter Eisenman
Project Architects: Thomas Leeser, Renato RIzzi, Peter Thaler
Architect-in-Charge: Thomas Leeser
Drawings: Raleigh Perkins, Susan Knauer, Edward Carroll, Alexis
Moser, Carlene Ramus, Joseph Rosa
Graphics: Charles Crawford, James Brown, Leslie Ryan
Models: Hiroshi Maruyama, Raleigh Perkins, Christine Chang, Donna
Cohen, Guillaume Ehrman, Rajip Erdem, Mara Graham, Kimberley
Hoyt, Marina Kieser, Jonathan Marvel, Michel Mossessian, David
Murphee, Fabio Nonis, Peter Robson, Adam Silver, Wolfgang
Tschapeller, Charles Barclay, Michael Casey

Master Plan for University Art Museum
California State University, Long Beach, California: 1986

Architect: Eisenman/Robertson Architects
Partner-in-Charge: Peter Eisenman
Associate-in-Charge: Thomas Leeser
Project Architects: Hiroshi Maruyama, Graeme Morland
Project Team: Michael Duncan, Manou Ernster, Judy Geib, Fabio
Ghersi, Frances Hsu, Christian Kohl, Paola Marzatico, Fabio Nonis, Joe
Tanney, Mark Wamble, Sarah Whiting, Gilly Youner
Gold Drawings: Mark Wamble
Landscape Architect: Hanna/Olin, Philadelphia

Biocentrum
J. W. Goethe University, Frankfurt am Main,
West Germany: 1986–87

Client: J. W. Goethe University
Architect: Eisenman/Robertson Architects
Partner-in-Charge: Peter Eisenman
Associate-in-Charge: Thomas Leeser
Project Team: Hiroshi Maruyama, David Biagi, Sylvain Boulanger, Ken
Doyno, Judy Geib, Holger Kleine, Christian Kohl, Frederic Levrat, Greg
Lynn, Carlene Ramus, Wolfgang Rettenmaier, Madison Spencer, Paul
Sorum, Sarah Whiting, David Youse
Mechanical Engineer: Augustine DiGiacomo (Jaros, Baum and Bolles)
Structural Engineer: Robert Silman (Silman Associates)
Landscape Architect: Laurie Olin (Hanna/Olin)
Artist: Michael Heizer
Color Consultant: Robert Slutzky

La Villette
Paris, France: 1987

Architects: Eisenman/Robertson Architects, Jacques Derrida, with
Renato Rizzi
Architects-in-Charge: Peter Eisenman, Jacques Derrida
Project Architects: Thomas Leeser, Renato Rizzi
Project Team: Franco Alloca, Paola Marzatico, Hiroshi Maruyama,
Manou Ernster

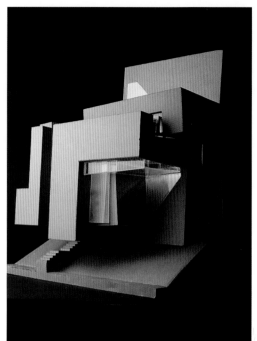

Carnegie-Mellon Research Institute
Pittsburgh, Pennsylvania: 1987–89

Client: Carnegie Mellon University, Richard M. Cyert, President; Frederick A. Rogers, Vice President, Business Affairs; William M. Kaufman, Vice President, Applied Research and Director, Mellon Institute; Sandra Hemingway, Director, Real Estate Development
Architect: Eisenman Architects
Principal-in-Charge: Peter Eisenman
Associate Principal-in-Charge: Richard N. Rosson
Project Team: Lawrence Blough, Kelly Hopkin, Richard Labonte, Greg Lynn, Marisabel Marratt, Mark Wamble, Joe Walter
Project Assistants: Wendy Cox, Simon Hubacher, Kim Tanzer, Nicolas Vaucher, Sarah Whiting, Katinka Zlonicky
Landscape Architect: Hanna/Olin, Ltd., Laurie Olin, Partner-in-Charge
Mechanical Engineer: Jaros, Baum & Bolles, Augustine DiGiacomo, Partner-in-Charge
Structural Engineer: Ove Arup & Partners, Guy Nordenson, Partner-in-Charge

Guardiola House
Cadiz, Spain: 1988

Client: D. Javier Guardiola
Principal-in-Charge: Peter Eisenman
Senior Associate-in-Charge: George Kewin
Associates-in-Charge: Thomas Leeser
Project Architect: Antonio Sanmartin
Project Team: Nuno Mateus, Jan Kleihues, Hiroshi Maruyama
Project Assistants: Begona Fernandez Shaw, Felipe Guardiola, Lise Anne Couture, Luis Rojo, Michael McInturf, Madison Spencer, Simon Hubacher, Maximo Victoria, Frederic Levrat, Anne Marx, Robert Choeff, Julie Shurtz, Dagmar Schimkus
Structural Engineer: Gerardo Rodriguez

Aronoff Center for Design and Art
University of Cincinnati, Cincinnati, Ohio: 1988–96

Client: University of Cincinnati, Joseph A. Steger, President; David L.McGirr, Vice President for Finance; Ronald B. Kull, Assistant Vice President and University Architect; Raymond D. Renner, Assistant Vice President and Director of Construction Management; Robert Yaun and John Childress, Project Managers; Jay Chatterjee, Dean; Joseph Power, AIA, Design Management Consultant
Architect: Eisenman Architects
Associate Architect: Lorenz & Williams, Inc.
Principals-in-Charge: Peter Eisenman, Richard Roediger, Jim Harrell
Associate Principals-in-Charge: George Kewin, Richard Rosson, Jerome Flynn
Project Architects: Donna Barry, Greg Lynn, Michael McInturf, Joseph Walter
Project Team: Lawrence Blough, Kelly Hopkin, Edward Mitchell, Astrid Perlbinder, Brad Winkeljohn (EA), Joseph Mitlo, Shari Rotella, Jerome Scott, James Schriefer, Michael Schuyler (LWI)
Project Assistants: Vincent Costa, Reid Freeman, Nazli Gonensay, Martin Houston, Richard Labonte, Corrine Nacinovic, Jean-Gabriel Neukomn, Karen Pollock, Joe Schott, Jim Wilson, Jason Winstanley, Leslie Young (EA)
Consultants: Construction: Dugan & Meyers, Inc.; Management: Francis Dugan, Daniel Dugan, Andy Englehart, Steve Klinder; Civil Engineer: United Consultants; Landscape Architect: Hargreaves Associates; Structural, Mechanical: Lorenz & Williams, Inc.; Acoustical: Jaffe Acoustics; Lighting: Fisher Marantz; Audio Visual: Boyce Nemec Designs Color Consultant: Donald Kaufman Color

Koizumi Sangyo Office Building
Tokyo, Japan: 1988–90

Client: Koizumi Sangyo Inc., Tokyo, Japan
Architect: Eisenman Architects, New York
Associate Architect: K Architects and Associates, Tokyo, Japan
Partners-in-Charge: Peter Eisenman, Kojiro Kitayama
Associate Partner-in-Charge: George Kewin
Project Architects: Hiroshi Maruyama (EA), Minoru Fujii (KA)
Project Team: Lawrence Blough, Robert Choeff, Lise Anne Couture, Begona Fernandez Shaw, Frederic Levrat, Dagmar Schimkus, Julie Shurtz, Mark Wamble (EA); Itaru Miyakawa, Tamihiro Motozawa, Hiroyuki Kubodera, Kazuhiro Isimaru, Susumu Arasaki, Yujiro Yamasaki (KA)

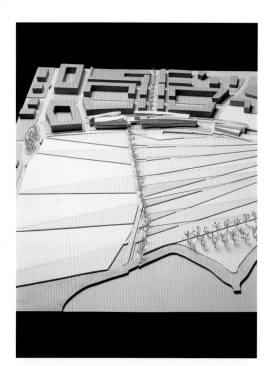

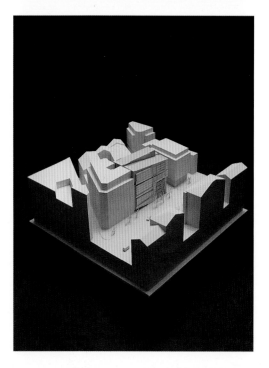

Banyoles Olympic Hotel
Banyoles, Spain: 1989

Client: Consorci Pel Desenvolupament De La Vila Olimpica, i Parc de la Draga; Pere Hernandez, President and Mayor of Banyoles; Joan Antoni Solans i Huguet, Vice President and Director General of Urbanism for the Generalitat de Catalunya; Joan Ignasi Coll i Olalla, Technical Director
Architect: Eisenman Architects
Principal-in-Charge: Peter Eisenman
Associate Principal-in-Charge: George Kewin
Associate Architect: Miquel Capdevila, Esteve Corominas
Project Designers: Begona Fernandez-Shaw, Nuno Mateus
Project Team: Ed Mitchell, Anne Peters, Weiland Vajen
Project Assistants: Lawrence Blough, John Durschinger, Kelly Hopkin, Martin Houston, Yuhang Kong, Richard Labonte, Mari Marratt, Tom Popoff, Henry Urbach, Joe Walter, Mark Wamble, Leslie Young
Structural Engineer: "Static" Ingenieria De Construccion, Gerardo Rodriguez

Groningen Music-Video Pavilion
Groningen, The Netherlands: 1990

Client: Groningen City Festival
Architect: Eisenman Architects
Principal-in-Charge: Peter Eisenman
Associate-in-Charge: George Kewin
Project Architect: Jorg Gleiter
Project Team: Andrea Stipa, Anton Viditz-Ward, Reid Freeman

Hotel Atocha 1-2-3
Madrid, Spain: 1990–93

Client: Sociedad Belga de Los Pinares De el Paular, Bruno Lecocq, Director and Chairman; Eric Lecocq, Director
Architect: Eisenman Architects
Associate Architect: The Austin Company, S.A.
Principals-in-Charge: Peter Eisenman, F.E."Brownie" Higgs
Associate Principal-in-Charge: George Kewin
Project Managers: David Koons, Jesus Salgado Marques, Luis Guerrero
Project Architects: David Koons, Gregory Luhan, Jorg Gleiter, John Curran, Nuno Mateus, Mark Searls, Antonio de la Morena, M. Magdalena Velez, Ramon Jose Farinas
Project Team: Mary Marratt, Andrea Stipa, Joe Walter, Jason Winstanley, Donald Skinner, John Maze, Tom Gilman, Andrew Burmeister
Project Assistants: Donna Barry, Rosa-Maria Colina, Brooks Critchfield, Angelo Directo, Winka Dubbledam, John Durschinger, Martin Felsen, Brad Gildea, Christophe Guinard, Jan Hinrichs, Brad Khouri, Andre Kikoski, Robert Kim, Justin Korhammer, Alexander Levi, Luc Leveque, Frederic Levrat, James McCrery, Gregory Merryweather, David Moore, Maureen Murphy-Ochsner, Karim Musfy, Alex Nussbaumer, Karen Pollock, Stefania Rinaldi, Raquel Sendra, Jody Sheldon, Marc Stotzer, Masahiro Suzuki, David Swanson, Thor Thors
Structural Engineer: The Austin Company, S.A., Fernando De La Frost, Fernando Yandela Terrosa
Contractor: The Austin Company S.A.

Nunotani Headquarters Building
Tokyo, Japan: 1990–92

Client: Nunotani Co., Ltd., Isayuki Nunotani, President; Hideki Kaya, Client Contact; Hideo Ueda, Chief Designer
Architect: Eisenman Architects
Principal-in-Charge: Peter Eisenman
Associate-in-Charge: George Kewin
Project Architect: Mark Wamble
Project Team: David Trautman, John Curran
Project Assistants: Thor Thors, Hans-Georg Berndsen, Karen Pollock, David Johnson, Evan Yassy, Gregory Merryweather, Andrea Stipa, Jason Winstanley, Andre Kikoski, Luc Levesque
Construction Manager and Contractor: The Zenitaka Corporation, Yoshimichi Hama, Director Manager; Yoshiteru Kagikawa, Director; Keiichi Kuwana, Deputy Manager

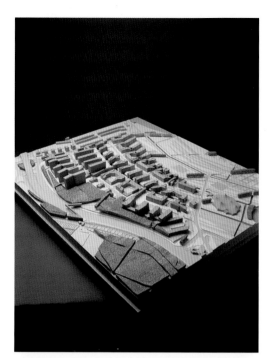

Greater Columbus Convention Center
Columbus, Ohio: 1989–93

Client: Franklin County Convention Facilities Authority, Claire Sawaya Hazucha, Executive Director; Client Representative: The Galbreath Company, James N. Hays
Architect: Eisenman Architects
Associate Architect: Richard Trott and Partners Architects, Inc.
Principals-in-Charge: Peter Eisenman, Richard Trott, Jean Gordon, Mike Burkey
Associate-in-Charge: Richard Rosson
Project Managers: Tracy Aronoff, Philip Babb, Thomas Ingledue
Project Architects: Mark Wamble, Jerome Scott, Thomas Leeser
Project Team: Madison Spenser, Richard Labonte, Kathleen Meyer, Dean Maltz, David Trautman, Lewis Jacobsen, Joe Walter, Nuno Mateus (EA); Jerry Kehlmeier, David Goth, Lu Schubert, Kristina Ennis, Tim Decker, John Meegan, Dave Reltenwald, Blaide Lewis, James Dean, George Van Neil, Carol Hummel, Chun Shin, Karen McCoy, Al Brook (RTPA)
Project Assistants: Yvhang Kong, John Durschinger, John Curran, Chiara Scortecci, Ilkka Tarkkanen, Jon Malis, Andres Viditz-Ward, Giovanni Rivolta, Francesca Acerboni, Jason Winstanley, John Juryj, Daniel Perez, Andres Blanco (EA)
Consultants: Engineer: Lorenz & Williams, Inc.; Civil Engineer: Moody/Nolan, Ltd.; Code: Oregon Group Architects; Roofing: Simpson, Gumperts & Heger, Inc.; Graphic Design: Mayer/Reed; Lighting: Jules Fisher & Paul Marantz,Inc.; Acoustics: Jaffe Acoustics, Inc. Construction Manager: Turner/Smoot/Zunt

Alteka Office Building
Tokyo, Japan: 1991

Client: Alteka Corporation, Tokyo, Japan
Architect: Eisenman Architects
Principal-in-Charge: Peter Eisenman
Associate Principal-in-Charge: Richard Rosson
Project Architect: Mark Wamble
Project Team: Gregory Merryweather, Nazli Gononsay
Project Assistants: Mina Mei-Szu Chow, Rosa-Maria Colina, Cornelius Deckert, Robert Kim, Maria Laurent, Frederic Levrat, Pierre-Olivier Milanini, Hadrian Predock, Jason Winstanley

Rebstockpark Master Plan
Frankfurt, Germany: 1990–94

Client: City of Frankfurt, Dieter Bock, and Buropark an der Frankfurter Messe GdR
Architect: Eisenman Architects
Associate Architect: Albert Speer & Partner GmbH
Landscape Architect: Hanna/Olin, Ltd., Laurie Olin, Shirley Kressel, Matthew W. White
Associate Landscape Architect: Boedeker, Wagenfeld, Niemeyer & Partners
Traffic Planning: Durth Roos Consulting GmbH
Principals-in-Charge: Peter Eisenman, Albert Speer, Laurie Olin
Associate Principals-in-Charge: George Kewin, Gerhard Brand
Project Managers: Norbert Holthausen, Michael Denkel, Shirley Kressel, Karina Aicher
Project Architects: Joachim Bothe, Jorg Gleiter, Nuno Mateus, Mark Wamble, Matthew White
Project Team: Pornchai Boonsom, Brad Gildea, Judith Haase, Justin Korhammer, Luc Levesque, Gregory Merryweather, Steven Meyer, Karim Musfy, Andrea Stipa, Marc Stotzer, Jason Winstanley, Corinna Wydler
Project Assistants: Donna Barry, Rosa-Maria Colina, John Curran, John Durschinger, Michael Eastwood, Carolina Garcia, Nazli Gononsay, John Juryj, Andre Kikoski, Stephano Libardi, Greg Lynn, James McCrery, Edward Mitchell, Jean Nukomn, Karen Pollock, Jon Stephens
Models: Eisenman Architects

Center for the Arts
Emory University, Atlanta, Georgia: 1991

Client: Emory University, Billy E. Frye, Interim President and Provost; John L. Temple, Executive Vice President; David Bright, Dean of Emory College; Maxwell L. Anderson, Director, 1996 Arts Initiative; Russell Seagren, Director of Campus Planning; Earle Whittington, Project Manager
Architect: Eisenman Architects
Principal-in-Charge: Peter Eisenman
Associate Principal-in-Charge: Richard Rosson
Project Manager: Tracy Aronoff
Project Architects: Selim Koder, Frédéric Levrat, Mark Searls
Project Team: Philip Babb, James Gettinger, Brad Gildea, Timothy Hyde, Richard Labonte, Ingel Liou, Gregory Luhan, James Luhur, James McCrery, Maureen Murphy-Ochsner, Lindy Roy, David Schatzle, Joseph Walter
Project Assistants: Ted Arleo, Donna Barry, Federico Beulcke, Sergio Bregante, Marc Breitler, Winka Dubbeldam, Daniel Dubowitz, John Durschinger, David Eisenmann, Abigail Feinerman, Ralf Feldmeier, Martin Felsen, Sigrid Geerlings, Robert Holton, Keelan Kaiser, Patrick Keane, James Keen, Brad Khouri, Rolando Kraeher, Joseph Lau, Maria Laurent, Vincent LeFeuvre, Claudine Lutolf, John Maze, Mark McCarthy, Steven Meyer, Julien Monfort, David Moore, Yayoi Ogo, Debbie Park, Axel Rauenbusch, Ali Reza Razavi, Mirko Reinecke, Tilo Ries, Stefania Rinaldi, David Ruzicka, Setu Shah, Tod Slaboden, Giovanni Soleti, Lucas Steiner, Helene Van gen Hassend, Marcus Wallner, Benjamin Wayne, Lois Weinthal, Erin Vali, Irina Verona
Consultants: Landscape Architect: Hanna/Olin, Ltd.; Structural: Stanley D. Lindsey & Associates, Inc.; Mechanical & Electrical: Nottingham, Brook & Pennington, Inc.; Acoustical: Kirkegaard & Associates, Inc.; Theater and Lighting: Theatre Projects Consultants, Inc. Cost: Donnell Consultants, Inc.

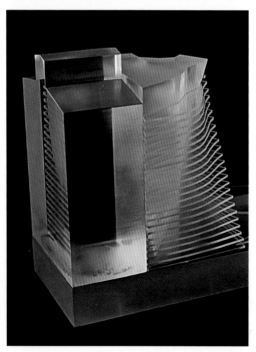

Max Reinhardt Haus
Berlin, Germany: 1992

Client: Advanta Management AG, Dieter Bock; OSTINVEST, Klaus-Peter Junge, Dieter Klaus
Architect: Eisenman Architects
Principal-in-Charge: Peter Eisenman
Associate Principal-in-Charge: George Kewin
Project Architects: Edward Mitchell, Lindy Roy, Richard Labonte
Project Team: Armand Biglari, Brad Gildea, Norbert Holthausen, Gregory Luhan, Stefania Rinaldi, David Schatzle, Jon Stephens
Project Assistants: Federico Beulcke, Mark Bretler, Andrew Burmeister, Robert Holten, Patrick Keane, Brad Khouri, Joseph Lau, Vincent LeFeuvre, Fabian Lemmel, John Maze, Steven Meyer, Debbie Park, Silke Potting, Benjamin Wade
Consultants: Landscape Architect: Hanna/Olin, Ltd.; Color Consultant: Donald Kaufman Color; Structural Engineer: Severud Associates; Mechanical Engineer: Jaros, Baum & Bolles; Wind & Shadow Studies: Spacetec Datengewinnung, Freiburg, Germany; Cost Estimating: Donnell Consultants, Inc.
Computer Images: Edward Keller

Nordliches Derendorf Master Plan Competition
Düsseldorf, Germany: 1992

Client: City of Dusseldorf Planning Department
Urban Designers: Eisenman Architects and Hanna/Olin, Ltd.
Principals-In-Charge: Peter Eisenman, Laurie Olin
Associates-in-Charge: George Kewin, Shirley Kressel
Project Architects: Winka Dubbledam, Norbert Holthausen, Donna Barry (EA); Matthew White (H/O)
Project Team: Edgar Cozzio, James Gettinger, Brad Gildea, Jorg Lesser, Jon Stephens, James McCrery
Project Assistants: Barbera Aderbeauer, Armand Biglari, Frederico Buelcke, Andy Burmeister, John Durschinger, Martin Felsen, Patrick Keane, Brad Khouri, Selim Koder, Fabian Lemmel, Frédéric Levrat, Gregory Luhan, Maureen Murphy-Ochsner, Stephania Rinaldi, Lindy Roy, David Schatzle (EA); Bobbie Huffman, David Rubin, Howard Supnik, Karen Skafte (H/O)
Traffic Planning: Durth Roos Consulting, Hans-Joachim Fischer
Color Consultants: Donald Kaufman Color, Donald Kaufman, Taffy Dahl
Computer Modeling: Mathematica Program, Seamus Moran, Physicist

Haus Immendorff
Düsseldorf, Germany: 1993

Client: Professor Jorg Immendorff
Architect: Eisenman Architects
Principal-in-Charge: Peter Eisenman
Associate-in-Charge: George Kewin
Project Architect: Lindy Roy
Project Team: David Schatzle, Patrick Keane, James Luhur
Project Assistants: Barbara Adabauer, Ted Arleo, Marc Bretler, Andrew Burmeister, Chi Yi Chang, Winka Dubbeldam, David Eisenmann, Abigail Feinerman, Annette Kahler, Fabian Lemmel, Jung Kue Liou, Gregory Luhan, Max Muller, Mirko Reinecke, Tilo Ries, Lucas Steiner
Construction Management: Phillip Holzmann HOG
Structural Engineer: Severud Associates
Mechanical, Plumbing, Electrical: Jaros Baum & Bolles

Regional Music Conservatory and Contemporary Arts Center
Site Francis Poulenc, Tours, France: 1993–94

Client: City of Tours
Architect: Eisenman Architects
Principal-in-Charge: Peter Eisenman
Associate Architect: Jean Yves Barrier Architecte
Design Consultant: Silvia Kolbowski
Associate Principal: George Kewin
Project Architect: Frédéric Levrat
Project Team: Helena Van gen Hassend, Will Meyer, Claudine Lutolf, Janine Washington, Alexandra Ligotti

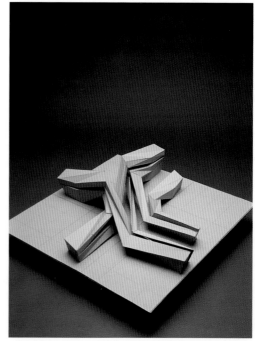

Klingelhöfer Housing
Berlin, Germany: 1995

Architect: Eisenman Architects
Principal-in Charge: Peter Eisenman
Associate-in-Charge: Richard Rosson
Project Architects: Sergio Bregante, Oliver Lang
Project Team: Diana Ibrahim, Setu Shah
Project Assistants: Hervé Biele, Gustavo Calazans, Stan Dorin, Jean-Cédric de Foy, Silke Haupt, Ingel Liou, Magdalena Miladovski, Yasmin Nicoular, Celine Parmentier, Mauricio Virgens

Monument and Memorial Site Dedicated to the Jewish Victims of the Nazi Regime in Austria 1938-1945
Vienna, Austria: 1995

Architect: Eisenman Architects
Design Consultant: Silvia Kolbowski
Principal-in-Charge: Peter Eisenman
Associate-in-Charge: Richard Rosson
Project Architects: Sergio Bregante, Diana Ibrahim
Project Assistants: Jean-Cedric de Foy, Stanislas Dorin, Chris Garcia, Silke Haupt, Matthias Hollwich, Magdalena Miladowski, Yasmin Nicoucar, Celine Parmentier, Boris Paschotta, Ian Weisse

Church for the Year 2000
Rome, Italy: 1996

Architect: Eisenman Architects
Principal-in-Charge: Peter Eisenman
Associate-in-Charge: Richard Rosson
Project Architects: Sergio Bregante, Diana Ibrahim
Project Assistants: Massimiliano Bosio, Stanislas Dorin, Lars Filmann, Jean-Cédric de Foy, Matthias Hollwich, Yasmin Nicoucar, Elisa Rosana Orlanski, Boris Paschotta, Celine Parmentier, Maria-Rita Perbellini, Matteo Pericoli, Christian Pongratz, Ingeborg Rocker, Olaf Schmidt, Susanne Sturm, Bettina Stolting, Martin Ulliana, Selim Vural, Ian Weisse

BFL Software, Ltd. Headquarters Building
Bangalore, India: 1996

Architect: Eisenman Architects
Principal-in-Charge: Peter Eisenman
Associate-in-Charge: Richard Rosson
Project Architects: Sergio Bregante, Heather Roberge, Kiran Venkatesh
Project Assistants: Luca Galofaro, Diana Giambiagi, Jan Henrik Hansen, Nikola Jarosch, Jörg Kiesow, Peter Lopez, Georg Mahnke, Philipp Mohr, MariaRita Perbellini, Sven Pfeiffer, Bernd Pflumm, Marco Pirone, Christian Pongratz, Ingeborg Rocker, Selim Vural

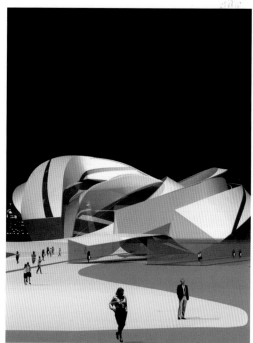

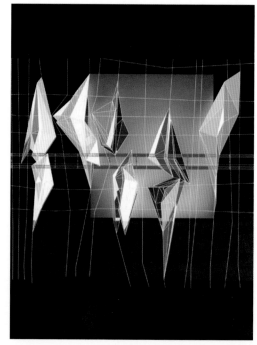

Bibliothèque de L'Institut Universitaire de Hautes Études Internationales
Geneva, Switzerland: 1996–97

Architect: Eisenman Architects
Associate Architect: ARX-Genève
Principals-in-Charge: Peter Eisenman, Frédéric Levrat
Associate-in-Charge: Richard Rosson
Project Designer: Rolando Kraeher
Project Team: Jean-Cédric de Foy, Diana Giambiagi
Project Assistants: Kristina Cantwell, Mats Edlund, Jan-Henrik Hansen, Sang-Wook Jin, Rasmus Joergensen, Jan Jurgens, Gwendolyn Kerschbaumer, Jörg Kiesow, Peter Lopez, Greg Luhan, Sebastian Mittendorfer, Michael Muroff, Sven Pfeiffer, MariaRita Perbellini, Christian Pongratz, Claire Sà, Patrick Salomon, Michael Schmidt, rainer Scholz, Angelika Solleder, Matthias Suchert, Lisa Torris, Selim Vural, Robert Wetzels, Markus Witta

Staten Island Institute of Arts and Sciences
New York, New York: 1997–present

Client: Staten Island Institute of Arts and Sciences: Dianne Powers, Chair, Board of Trustees; Bonnie Nalwasky, Interim Director
Architect: Eisenman Architects
Principal-in-Charge: Peter Eisenman
Associate-in-Charge: Richard Rosson
Project Manager: Tracy Aronoff
Project Designer: Ingeborg Rocker
Project Assistants: Yolanda do Campo, Juliette Cezzar, Adriana Cobo, Jean-Cédric de Foy, Marco Galofaro, Diana Giambiagi, Nicholas Haagensen, Jan-Henrik Hansen, Bart Hollanders, Chien-Ho Hsu, Claire Hyland, Sang-Wook Jin, Rolando Kraeher, Abhijeet Lakhia, Dirk Lellau, Peter Lopez, Gianluca Milesi, Sebastian Mittendorfer, Michael Morrow, Michael Muroff, Christi Raber, Heather Roberge, Ingeborg Rocker, Claire Sà, Patrick Salomon, Stephan Schoeller, Oliver Schütte, Urban Stirnberg, Selim Vural

The Virtual House
Berlin, Germany: 1997

Architect: Eisenman Architects
Principal-in-Charge: Peter Eisenman
Associate-in-Charge: Richard Rosson
Project Designer: Ingeborg Rocker
Project Team: Lloyd Huber, Bernd Pflumm, Heather Roberge, Selim Vural
Project Assistants: Emanuela Alessandri, Adriana Cobo, Jan-Henrik Hansen, Nikola Jarosch, Sang-Wook Jin, Rasmus Joergensen, Bernard Kormoss, Abhijeet Lakhia, Peter Lopez

Illinois Institute of Technology Student Center Competition
Chicago, Illinois: 1998

Architect: Eisenman Architects
Principal-in-Charge: Peter Eisenman
Associate-in-Charge: Richard Rosson
Project Designer: Ingeborg Rocker
Project Assistants: Yolanda do Campo, Juliette Cezzar, Jon Dillon, Marco Galofaro, Nicholas Haagensen, Bart Hollanders, Chien-ho Hsu, Bernard Kormoss, Scott Larsen, Lawrence McDonald, Claire Sà, Oliver Schütte, Stephan Schoeller, Urban Stirnberg, Selim Vural, Paul de Voe, Karen Weber
Landscape Architect: Olin Partnership: Laurie Olin
Structural Engineer: Büro Happold G.m.b.H.: Craig Schwitter, Andre Cheszar
MPE Engineers and Acoustical Consultants: Cosentini Associates: Marvin Mass

INTERIORITY   **EXTERIORITY**

	House I	House II	House III	House IV	House VI	House X	House 11a	Cannaregio	House El Even Odd	Berlin IBA Housing	Fin d' Ou T Hous	Wexner Center	Romeo and Juliet	Long Beach	Biocentrum	La Villette	CMRI	Casa Guardiola	Aronoff Center	Koizumi Sangyo
FORMAL TOOLS																				
extrusion																				
twisting																				
extension																				
interweaving																				
displacement																				
disassembling																				
shear																				
morphing																				
interference																				
intersection																		◣		
projection									◣											
torquing																				
distortion																				
superposition														◢	◢	◢				
nesting						◣		◣				◣				◢				
warping																			◣	
repetition								◢							◢		◣		◣	
shifting	◣																			
scaling											◢		◢							
imprinting							◢											◢	◢	
slippage				◢																
transformation	◣			◢																
rotation			◢													◢				
doubling	◣	◣														◢				
CONCEPTUAL TOOLS																				
inversion					◣															
mapping									◢			◢	◢							
artificial excavation									◣				◣	◢						
folding																				
grafting																			◢	◢
tracing						◢		◢										◢	◢	◢
marking	◣																			
layering	◢		◢																	
montage				◢											◢					
voiding																	◣			
decomposition						◢														
blurring																			◣	
striation																				
gridding								◢												
laminar flow																				

Projects (columns, left to right):

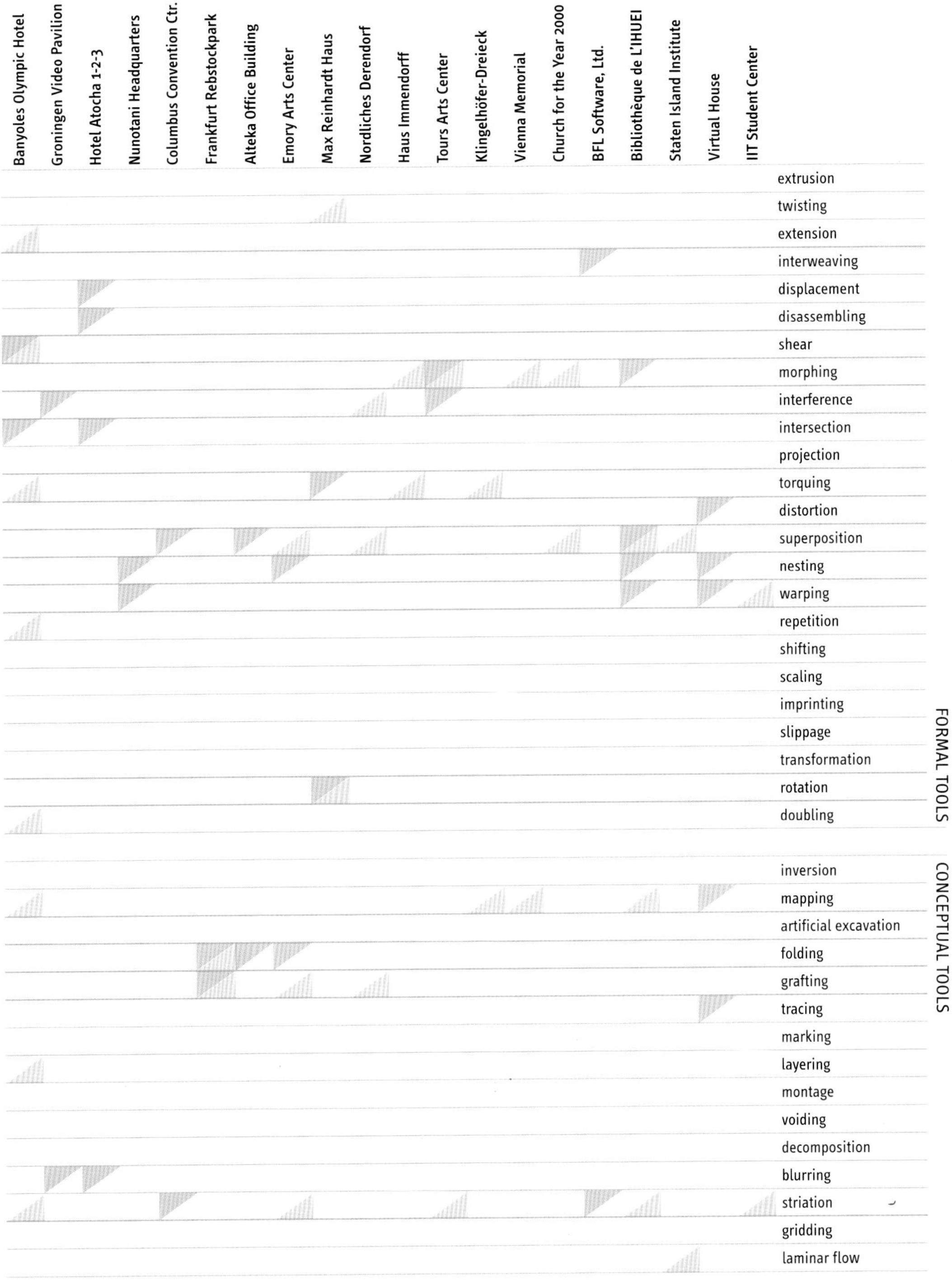

1. Banyoles Olympic Hotel
2. Groningen Video Pavilion
3. Hotel Atocha 1-2-3
4. Nunotani Headquarters
5. Columbus Convention Ctr.
6. Frankfurt Rebstockpark
7. Alteka Office Building
8. Emory Arts Center
9. Max Reinhardt Haus
10. Nordliches Derendorf
11. Haus Immendorff
12. Tours Arts Center
13. Klingelhöfer-Dreieck
14. Vienna Memorial
15. Church for the Year 2000
16. BFL Software, Ltd.
17. Bibliothèque de L'IHUEI
18. Staten Island Institute
19. Virtual House
20. IIT Student Center

FORMAL TOOLS

- extrusion
- twisting
- extension
- interweaving
- displacement
- disassembling
- shear
- morphing
- interference
- intersection
- projection
- torquing
- distortion
- superposition
- nesting
- warping
- repetition
- shifting
- scaling
- imprinting
- slippage
- transformation
- rotation
- doubling

CONCEPTUAL TOOLS

- inversion
- mapping
- artificial excavation
- folding
- grafting
- tracing
- marking
- layering
- montage
- voiding
- decomposition
- blurring
- striation
- gridding
- laminar flow

239

Peter Eisenman is an architect and educator. In 1980, after many years of teaching, writing and producing respected theoretical work, he established his professional practice to focus exclusively on building. He has designed a wide range of prototypical projects, including large-scale housing and urban design projects, innovative facilities for educational institutions, and a series of inventive private houses.

In 1993, opening ceremonies were held for the $65 million Convention Center in Columbus, Ohio, and in 1996 for the $35 million Aronoff Center for Design and Art. In 1985, Mr. Eisenman received a Stone Lion (First Prize) for his Romeo and Juliet project at the Third International Architectural Biennale in Venice. Mr. Eisenman was one of the two architects to represent the United States at the Fifth International Exhibition of Architecture of the Venice Biennale in 1991, and his projects are exhibited at museums and galleries around the world. Mr. Eisenman was the founder and former director of the Institute for Architecture and Urban Studies, an international think-tank for architectural criticism. He has received numerous awards, including a Guggenheim Fellowship, the Brunner Award of the American Academy of Arts and Letters, and a grant from the National Endowment for the Arts.

His academic involvement has included teaching at Cambridge University, Princeton University, Yale University, Ohio State University, and the University of Arkansas. From 1982 to 1985, he was the Arthur Rotch Professor of Architecture at Harvard University, and in the fall of 1993 he was the Eliot Noyes Visiting Design Critic at Harvard. Currently he is the first Irwin S. Chanin Distinguished Professor of Architecture at The Cooper Union in New York City and a visiting professor at Princeton University.

Mr. Eisenman received a Bachelor of Architecture degree from Cornell University, a Master of Architecture degree from Columbia University, M.A. and Ph.D. degrees from the University of Cambridge, and honorary Doctor of Fine Arts degrees from the University of Illinois–Chicago and Pratt Institute.

Photo credits

All model photos: Dick Frank, with the exception of Long Beach (Michael Moran), Max Reinhardt Haus (Jochen Littkemann), and Vienna Memorial (Hertha Hurnaus).
Houses I, II, III and VI: Dick Frank
Berlin IBA Housing: Reinhard Goerner
Wexner Center, Aronoff Center, and Columbus Convention Center: Jeff Goldberg (ESTO)
Koizumi Sangyo, Nunotani Headquarters: Shigeo Ogawa